Warriors
Are Like
Pearls
and
Biscuits

Sherry-Marie Perguson

WESTBOW
PRESS®
A DIVISION OF THOMAS NELSON
& ZONDERVAN

WestBow Press books may be ordered through
booksellers or by contacting:

WestBow Press
A Division of Thomas Nelson & Zondervan
1663 Liberty Drive
Bloomington, IN 47403
www.westbowpress.com
1 (866) 928-1240

ISBN: 978-1-9736-9465-6 (sc)
ISBN: 978-1-9736-9466-3 (hc)
ISBN: 978-1-9736-9464-9 (e)

Library of Congress Control Number: 2020911648

Print information available on the last page.

WestBow Press rev. date: 6/27/2020

A warrior princess needs her sword for battle, but her armor is not complete until she dons her pearls. Sherry-Marie's southern roots, once again, shine forth with unfaltering faith, pearls of wisdom, encouragement, Sherryisms, humor, and sassiness, all of which makes her storytelling style so unique.

This Book Is Dedicated To

My readers, many of whom have become cherished friends and who walk with me on my journey.

My husband, who is a constant, encouraging, and loving support to me. I love him with all my heart.

Jesus, who loves me in spite of myself.

You all make me who I am. Thank you for loving me.

Contents

Introduction

*It is to your advantage not only to
be doing what you began and were
desiring to do a year ago, but now
you also must complete the doing of
it. (2 Corinthians 8:10 NKJV)*

As I once again became aware of the nudging
of the Lord to write another book, I ran across
this scripture. It kept repeating in my head and
resonating. It was like my brain was telling me,
*There is an item on your to-do list that needs to
be addressed.* When something is ordained of the
Lord, you will not be able to shake it off, so let's
finish the work, warriors.

Revelation says, "He who was seated on the
throne said, 'Look, I am making everything new.'
Then He said, 'Write this down, for what I tell you
is trustworthy and true'" (Revelation 21:5 NIV).

Don't you just love those God moments

where after reading His Word, He speaks to you personally and says, *Write this down*? I do. I love the moments when He takes time out of His extremely busy schedule to meet with me—one on one—and to tell me, *Write this down*. I have made a list of promises that He is going to bring to pass because He cannot lie, and He told me to write it down.

As both a writer and a child of God, I don't take it lightly when the Lord speaks to me. I desire to be obedient in what He is calling me to do. If He tells me write it down, I will do my best to write it down, regardless of what He desires me to write.

There are over forty (probably more, but this is how many I have counted) verses in the Bible about writing things down.

> The Lord instructed Moses, "Write this down on a permanent reminder." (Exodus 17:14 NLT)

> "Thus speaks the Lord God of Israel saying: Write in a book for yourself all the words that I have spoken to you." (Jeremiah 30:2 NKJV)

This same instruction applies to all of us. You may not have been called to write a book, but when after reading your Bible, God speaks words of life and promise to you, you need to write them down. Buy a journal and begin to listen to what God is saying to you because He wants to tell you how much He loves you. He wants to tell you how much He cares. He wants to give you His personal promises. He wants you to study to learn more about Him. Do your homework. Write it down.

When things get a little out of hand in your world, you can go back to your personal journal or notebook and read the promise that God gave *you*. He is a personal God. Write it down.

Proverbs 7:3 reads, "Bind them on your fingers; Write them on the tablet of your heart," (NKJV). Remember how you were taught to tie a string on your finger to help you remember something you were supposed to do? It's the same thing here, warriors. God wants us to tie strings on our fingers and to remember what He says.

Did you know that your heart has a tablet? Well it does. God says so. Because God mentions it and instructs us to write on it, it must surely mean that it is important to Him. But what does that mean? It means, that we should remember it. We should memorize it. It is important. You will need to know it somewhere down the line.

There have been times when I have argued with myself. I have thought, *What makes me*

think anyone would want to read what I write?
Why would anyone receive encouragement from
me? I can really be brutal to me. I can make me
feel pretty unworthy very quickly. I can bring up
all the old hurts and mistakes. I can bring up the
failures and embarrassments. Oh believe me, I'm
good at it.

Just ask my sister. She will tell you that I
throw pity parties now and then. When I do, she
invariably tells me, "Don't go there, Sis. Don't
beat yourself up. Guilt is of the devil. God doesn't
remember. He forgives and doesn't hold it up to
us anymore."

So when I'm finished telling myself all the
reasons why I shouldn't, God shouts at me. Yes,
sometimes He shouts because I'm stubborn,
and like any good parent, He is tired of my
complaining, and He wants to get my attention
for a reason. Lately, He has been shouting.

When He shouts, He tells me, *Why not you?*
Why not? You have experienced the deepest lows.
You have walked that part of the journey—the
journey of hurt, sadness, and loneliness. Why not
you? That's why I placed this calling upon you.
If I say you can do this, who are you to argue
with Me?

"One step of obedience positions us for an incredible journey."
~ a Sherryism

Okay, so here I am again. I hope this new book lifts your spirit when you are feeling down, causes you to laugh out loud and to shake your head, gives you a desire to bake something yummy, and encourages you to not only pick up your sword for the battle but also to put on your pearls and react like a biscuit. You know what to do. Grab your blankie, get all comfy, and have your favorite beverage nearby. Then let's get started on the journey. I can't wait.

Chapter 1

From an Irritant to a Pearl

"No grit, no pearl". ~ Author unknown

The making of a pearl begins with an irritant—really. Particles from the ocean become lodged inside of the oyster. Some people think it is a particle of sand, but more likely than not, it is just a piece of debris that is floating along in the water. Out of its will to protect itself and survive, the oyster surrounds the irritant with a protective layer of cells, which make up the pearl sack. The sack begins to produce layers of a glue-like substance called nacre. The irritant keeps getting coated with layer after layer of this substance, which forms thc pcarl and polishes it to perfection.

But we must remember that the oyster had to go through physical pain and injury in order to produce the pearl. So, is the pearl a wound or a scar? I would say that a pearl is the healing of an injury. We should learn this valuable lesson from the oyster. When life throws its worst irritants at us, we should take them on and cover them with layers and layers of the Word of God. We should make that thing, which was brought to us, irritates us, and even destroys us, into a thing of beauty, a pearl or a battle scar, if you will.

Just like pearls, we are all unique. No two pearls are alike, and neither are we, dear warriors. We are all so different, yet we are all so important, and yes, we are all needed. Never lose sight of who you are and the fact that someone needs you. Be willing to be true to yourself and to share *you* with those around you. God thought you were good enough to create, therefore, believe in what He created.

Just one pearl makes a lovely necklace, but if we string many pearls together, the necklace becomes even more beautiful. Let's back up a little and talk about some of the irritants that are brought into our lives and that bring about the pearl in us.

1. Fear

Fear is a big irritant. It can become debilitating very quickly. Sometimes, fear grows because we do not address what is causing us to experience this emotion. By not addressing it, fear will continue to grow and to torment us.

Fear can come from anywhere and everywhere. It can be anything from having a bad dream to believing someone is going to hurt you (physically and emotionally). You soon become afraid of everything. You don't want to go outside. You don't want to be around other people, not even loved ones. As the songwriters Zach Williams, Jonathan Smith, and Jason Ingram penned, "Fear is a liar."

A whisperer has the ability to calm others and to bring a sense of peace. There are all kinds of whisperers: horse whisperers, dog whisperers, buffalo whisperers, and lion whisperers. I even read of a man who was a skunk whisperer (bless his heart). But the most important whisperer is Jesus.

He is our soul whisperer. He is our storm whisperer. He comes to us in our storms, and He not only whispers to the storm, causing the wind and waves to subside and obey Him, but He also whispers to our souls. Then the anxiety and fear subside, and His peace overrides any situation that is meant to destroy us. I thank God for my soul and storm whisperer. So, warriors, when this irritant of fear comes, use your power of layering the Word of God onto it and shape your pearl.

2. Stress and Anxiety

Whew. Talk about irritating. I will be transparent here and tell you that I have experienced this firsthand and that it is quite bewildering. A few short months ago, I found myself in the ER. The diagnosis was an anxiety or panic attack. What? As I lay there listening to the doctor, I began to ask myself, *How did I get here?* Then I talked to Jesus, saying, *Lord, I'm your girl. I am a warrior. I should be better than this.*

I really began to search my heart. What was going on with me? Did this diagnosis make me any less of a warrior? No.

Nothing defines how the irritants of stress and anxiety grab hold of us and consume every nerve, every sense, and every thought. We all deal with some amount of stress daily because we all live in a very fast-paced and demanding world. Even if your job doesn't put demands on you, other people will. Eventually, you will begin to put demands upon yourself.

Warriors, if you are battling the helpless and unexplainable feelings of anxiety, panic, and stress, there is hope. Don't keep your head down. Lift it up in praise and thanksgiving to the Lord. Play your anointed Christ-centered music loudly. Read scripture out loud. Stand on the never-failing Word of God. Learn relaxation techniques that will calm down your nervous system. Never be ashamed that you battle these irritants and never consider yourself less a child of God when doing so. He loves us in spite of our weaknesses.

Second Corinthians 12:9 reads, "He said to them. My grace is sufficient for you, for my strength is made perfect in weakness" (NKJV). The NIV translation of that verse reads like this, "My grace is sufficient for you, for my *power* is made perfect in weakness." Chew on that today.

So when life places demands that bring stress and anxiety on you, remember this: Having a goal is great and is different from having a demand. A goal is something we work for. It may take days, weeks, or even years to achieve. We are okay with that. A demand, however, puts pressure on us to get it done and get it done *now*.

Stress and anxiety are irritants, but they do not have the power to destroy our pearls. When these irritants come, how do we take care of the injuries they cause? We must layer the power of God's Word over them. We are shaping our pearls. Again, what is happening to our pearls? The irritants of stress and anxiety are designed to destroy our pearls, but in reality, we are layering our beautiful pearls with the Word of God.

3. Sickness

Let me just say here and now that sickness is an incredible irritant. Whether we are fighting life-threatening battles or other physical issues, sometimes, we just can't seem to get victory over them. They are difficult irritants. Sickness constantly irritates our pearls and sometimes causes us to become weak and disheartened in our faith. Then this affects our attitude and joy, not to mention the toll that sickness has on our bodies.

Yet every time the irritant of sickness rubs against our pearls, guess what happens: The Word of God stands up to it, not only protecting our pearls but also polishing them. Sickness could be one of the strongest irritants in your life, but don't worry and don't give up.

With other irritants, we can sometimes control how long the injury from it will last and how severe the injury will become, but this is not true of sickness. Sickness is one of those irritants that has a lot of unknown parts to it. It's okay because claiming the Word of God over and over is like rubbing a soft cloth ever so gently to bring out the luster of our pearls.

4. Loss

Whether it's the loss of something—a home, material things, a job, a marriage—or the death of a loved one, no irritant is greater. Yet the stronger the irritant is, the greater the power of God's Word is as it layers over and over on it. We have been rubbing, protecting, shaping, and now polishing the luster of our pearls.

Let us not allow the loss of material things, the loss of a marriage, or the death of a loved one keep us from the love of the living. We must learn to look loss straight in the eye, and without batting an eyelash, we must speak the Word of God, even when our heart is broken.

When we walk around like zombies with no feelings and no desire to take a step forward, to laugh, or love, it's a crucial time for our pearls. Keep polishing until their luster is blinding and the glory of the Lord shines through in all its brilliance. That's when the injuries to our pearls will be healed.

It won't happen overnight. In fact, all these

irritants have taken close to a lifetime to shape our precious pearls. But that lifetime, layered with the Word of God, will produce pearls of great price.

Matthew 13:45–46 reads, "Again, the kingdom of heaven is like a merchant seeking beautiful pearls, who, when he had found one pearl of great price, went and sold all that he had and bought it" (NKJV). God sees you as His pearl of great price. He gave everything He had—His son, Jesus—to purchase you. Why? So He could have fellowship with you forever. Never be ashamed of the pearl that you are.

Let's just face it, becoming a pearl hurts. Sometimes, it hurts to grow. I vividly remember the summer I was twelve. I remember the color of my room, which was just a pale whisper of pink. I remember watching the beautiful Rose of Sharon bush in front of my bedroom window swaying in the warm summer breeze. That summer, my youngest sibling was born three days after my birthday.

Most of all, I remember the leg cramps I would get in the middle of the night. They were so severe that I would jump out of bed crying. It seemed to happen almost every night. *That* summer, I grew to my forever frame of five feet seven inches. It *hurt*, but I *grew*. Even when it hurts, you are still healthy and growing. Hang in there. You are polishing your pearl. Change can hurt.

How many of us pray, *Change me?* I have to be honest and tell you that sometimes, those two words scare me. Why? Because I am human, and being human, I am prone to getting into my comfort zone. I do not want to be changed, period. Maybe I can't see my need for change. Maybe I am afraid of what change may require of me. Maybe I'm just stubborn and want things my way. I don't have an exact or perfect answer as to why those two words scare me. But the reality is that if I want to grow, I have to endure change.

Every day brings about change in some way, whether it is subtle or abrupt. A child who never changes, never grows. A flower that never changes will die in the bud and never reveal its beauty. The caterpillar will never lift off the ground to fly as a new butterfly if it does not endure change. You get the picture.

Change will always happen, even if it scares us or we don't want it to happen. So today when we pray, *Lord change me*, let's get excited about what that may mean instead of dreading the process.

"How precious are your thoughts about me, O God. They cannot be numbered. I can't even count them; they outnumber the grains of sand." (Psalm 139:17–18 NLT)

I often wonder what God's precious thoughts are for me. He thinks of me more times than the number of grains of sand. Does He really love me that much? I think of my hubby *a lot* and pray blessings upon him. I think of my children almost constantly and always pray for them to have personal and real relationships with Jesus. I think of you, my faithful readers and friends, pray for your victories, and rejoice with you when those victories are manifested.

But unlike God's thoughts, my thoughts cannot be measured with grains of sand. How greatly He must love us—those precious thoughts of His. He loves us so much that He gave His only son, Jesus, to be the lamb that was sacrificed for our sins. How much does He think about us and love us? That much.

The sadness of the life not *taken* but *given* on that Good Friday remains the single most important event in history. It established a lifeline for each of us, no matter what the depth of our despair is. He gave up His life so that we could experience life everlasting. He was thinking of you that day. He was thinking of me. His thoughts were of us.

I, for one, will be overwhelmed with gratitude and humbleness when I see his nail-scarred hands and feet. I know that He had *us (me and you)* on His mind when He endured that horrific pain.

I know you have been through so much. We all have. We all have lots of scars. But *you* are so beautiful, even with those scars. You don't have to cover them. Embrace the struggle that brought them because you made it through. You have been healed, and you are continuing to heal. You are still able to stand, and you will continue to stand. Being victorious over your battles, even though you forever carry scars, brings hope to those who are traveling behind you. Never be ashamed of your scars. You are still here and standing. You have won.

Even though at times the memory of the struggle overwhelms you, *never, ever* allow it to suck you back into feelings of hurt, abandonment, and ugliness. Every day, you are growing into that beautiful miracle God always knew you were going to be. Begin to love you.

You are awesome. Don't allow the actions of others to play havoc with your heart, mind, and emotions. Rise above anything that makes you sad, disappointed, or hurt. It is not always an easy thing to do, but you can do it. The more you try, the easier it becomes. You may not be perfect, but you are brokenly awesome. You are that great pearl for which He sacrificed His very life.

Once, I heard an old story. The original storyteller is unknown. It goes like this:

> There was a group of women holding a Bible study. They began to study the book of Malachi. (Malachi is a small book in the Old Testament of the Bible.)
>
> They came across verse Malachi 3:3 (NLT), and it reads "He will sit like a refiner of silver." Many in the group did not understand what this verse meant. One of the women offered to find out about the process of refining silver and then report back to the group.
>
> She made an appointment with a silversmith to watch him work. As she watched the silversmith, he held a piece of silver over the fire and heated it up. He explained that in refining silver, you needed to hold the silver in the middle of the fire where the flames are the hottest. This burns away all the impurities.
>
> The woman thought about God holding us in our hot spot. Thinking of the

verse again, "that he sits as a refiner and purifier of silver". She asked the silversmith if it was true that he had to sit there in front of the hot fire the whole time the silver was being refined.

The man replied "yes". He told her that not only did he have to sit there holding the silver, but he had to keep his eyes on the silver the entire time while it was in the fire.

If the silver was left even a moment too long in the flames, it would be damaged.

The woman was silent, then she asked "How do you know when the silver is fully refined?"

The silversmith smiled at her and answered "Oh, that's easy. When I see my image in it."

Oh, this brought tears to my eyes. How many times have we felt like we were *right in the middle of the fire where the heat is the hottest*? All that time, we felt like we were alone—absolutely alone. Yet God, our silversmith, was sitting there right in front of us also in the heat. His eyes never left us. He watched with every bit of love and compassion that He owned. He made sure that we didn't stay in the fire a second longer than was needed so that we wouldn't be damaged. Then the special moment happened: when He could see His image in us. He very carefully removed us from the fire.

I am so unworthy of such love and compassion. I complain so much when I'm in the fire. I only need to realize that my silversmith will never drop me in the flames. He is only waiting to see His image in me. Praise the Lord today and forevermore.

I once saw an advertisement for sweatshirts. The sweatshirt made for moms read, "I'm a cool Mom, right?" and the sweatshirt made for children read, "Please stop talking." This advertisement made me laugh out loud. I know that the sweatshirt ad was meant to be funny (and it was). I know that it was meant to show that sometimes, we just embarrass our kids and ourselves.

But you know me; I can always find God in the moment. I began to think about how I must seem to God at times. I am all up in His face, praying, crying, and begging for something. I really try to make my case seem important or worthy enough for Him to take the time to fix.

In reality, He just wants to tell me, "Please stop talking. I've got this."

I lived most of my life trying to convince God to see and do things my way. Then one day, it hit me like a ton of bricks. I thought, *This really isn't working for me. Maybe I need to refocus on and relearn how to communicate with my Savior.*

We can arrive at a place on our journeys where we are no longer begging God to do our bidding. It is a place of unspeakable calm, reassurance, peace, and joy. It is surrounded by and engulfed in the knowledge that maybe what we want isn't the best thing for us, so we will step back and accept with open arms, the *good* things God has planned and will bring into our lives.

It's about the submission, not the petition. ~ a Sherryism

I thank God that I don't have to beg and plead. All I need to do is ask and believe.

There are things in my life that I covet and that will help my pearl glow and my silver shine.

- ✧ I covet and desire to live a blessed life.
- ✧ I covet that I will use up every talent the Lord gives me while I walk out my life's journey.

✧ I covet that I can share my rough days to others so that they can make it through.

✧ I covet that I will always show love, respect, and honor to my friends.

✧ I covet that my life, even though it's a vapor, will be used for God's glory.

✧ I covet that I will laugh for joy, knowing *who* I am and belong to.

✧ I covet that I will hold on to the promise that no weapon formed against me shall prosper.

✧ I covet that I will soak up the knowledge that I am blessed to be a blessing.

I covet all these things.

I once heard a quote that I like: "Follow your heart but take your brain with you" (author unknown). We all too often lead with our hearts because we are emotionally involved. We forget to take our brains. This can be an issue. We might think, *My heart knows the way*, and maybe it does, but we don't always consider the consequences.

For instance, I love fried chicken. I could easily be led by my love for fried chicken. I could eat it every day, all day. But somewhere along the line, if I don't use my brain and tell myself to eat the fried chicken in moderation, there's a good chance that I might develop high cholesterol. Do you see why we might want to use our hearts and brains together when we make decisions?

I want to end this chapter with a story that I once heard.

An old man was walking on the beach one morning after a storm. In the distance, he could see someone moving like a dancer. As he came closer, he saw that it was a young woman picking starfish and gently throwing them into the ocean.

He asked, "Young lady, why are you throwing starfish into the ocean?"

"The sun is up, and the tide is going out, and if I do not throw them in, they will die" she said.

He replied "But young lady, do you not realize that there are many miles of beach and thousands of starfish? You cannot possibly make a difference."

The young woman listened politely, then bent down, picked up another starfish and threw it into the sea. "It made a difference for that one." She said.

You can make a difference when you make the right choices.

Chapter 2

Choosing Your Battles

Praise be to the LORD my Rock who trains my hands for WAR; my fingers for BATTLE.
(Psalm 144:1 NIV)

I was talking to my dear friend Donna recently, and I was declaring an answer to prayer over her. Her response was, "From your mouth to God's ear." *Wow.* I thought, *Now that is childlike faith. The kind of faith God loves to hear His children speak.* Yes, it is *just* that simple: from our mouths to God's ear.

Not only once in a while but every day, God wants to have a conversation with us. He wants you and me to wake up and say, "Hello, Lord," and then communicate with Him as we would our dearest friend or loving parent because He is both. He has the same desire for you and me that He had for Adam and Eve. He wants to have a relationship with us.

I liken it to this. I desire for my children to call and text me every day. I love hanging out with them and doing things with them. I have one daughter who includes me in everything in her life, whether it's good or bad. It makes me feel loved and wanted. I love hearing what has happened during her day and what she is cooking for dinner. I know that I'm included in her everyday life.

Another daughter calls and texts me sporadically. She is always loving and respectful, but I don't feel that she opens up to me very much. I don't know much about what goes on in her personal life. She seems guarded. I know she loves me with all her heart. We both adore each other, but I'm not really included in her everyday stuff.

Another daughter usually only calls or texts me because of my reaching out to her or her needing something. I know she loves me, but it is usually only from a distance and if there is a need.

I am sure that most of us have different relationships with our children. This is how God sees us. Which relationship do you have with your Father God? Are you the one who includes Him in your life every day and communicates with Him all the time? Are you the one who sporadically thinks about talking to Him yet never tells Him anything? Do you have a casual relationship with Him, even though you really love Him? Are you the one who only talks to Him when you need something? Maybe you never just tell Him how much you love Him and how thankful you are that He is part of your life.

Maybe this year, our goal should be to communicate with God on a more personal, daily basis. Open the lines of communication, invite Him into your daily life, and allow Him to interrupt, rearrange, and redirect you on your journey (Just a funny note here. This morning, I was texting on my cell phone. I thought I typed, "saith the Lord," but my auto correct changed it to "Saute the aloes." Ha ha. Yes, correct communication is *very* important).

We must realize that the answer to our prayer does not hinge on how eloquently we pray or how long the prayer is. It does not come because we know exactly how to pray. We may not have a clue how to pray or what to pray for. The answer lies in God, period. He just wants us to talk to Him. Talk to Him and love Him. That is all.

Are you believing for and expecting a miracle? I once heard that you have to replace your fear with faith. We carry many fears, and much of the time, we do not even realize it. We fear the unknown—that is a biggie. We fear abandonment, ridicule, and loss—of love, finances, and health. Do you see a pattern here? Fears are associated with loss, which breeds sadness and hopelessness.

But faith is totally the opposite. It *thrives* on the unknown. It brings about peace, calmness, hope, and a vision of good things.

When *fear* begins to grip your mind, heart, and spirit, make a conscious effort to replace it with *faith*. Begin to exercise your faith, and it will grow stronger. It's just like when you exercise weak muscles. Daily exercise begins to strengthen your muscles, and change happens. In the gym, there are resistance bands. A resistance band is an elastic band used for strength training. They are used most frequently during physical therapy and rehabilitation from an injury. They allow the slow rebuilding of strength.

James 4:7 reads, "Therefore submit to God. *Resist* the devil and he will flee from you" (NKJV). God knows how important it is to resist the devil, to daily exercise our spiritual man, to feed him faith, and to overcome fear.

Sometimes, we must realize that we are not

in a battle with flesh and blood "but against principalities, against powers, against the rulers of darkness of this world, against spiritual wickedness" (Ephesians 6:12 KJV). We aren't fighting humans, but we are fighting spirits. The enemy must be fought by praying, fasting, speaking the Word of God, and claiming your right and inheritance as a child of God.

Don't cower and back down in defeat. There is victory ahead. Your enemy knows the Word of God. He knows the power that you possess when you yield yourself to God and stand on His promises. I don't care what your battlefield looks like. God wins.

But you have a choice. You can play along with the enemy in a poor-me stance, or you can fall upon your knees and bombard heaven. Then get up, shake yourself off, and begin to read the Word of God out loud to the enemy of your soul and of your family's soul.

First Peter 5:8 says, "Stay alert. Watch out for your great enemy, the devil. He prowls around like a roaring lion, looking for someone to destroy." Then verses 9–10 go on to say, "But stand <u>firm</u> against him. Be <u>strong</u> in your faith and remember that your Christian brothers and sisters all over the world are going through the same thing you are." (NLT)

Don't give in. Don't give up. Go get your victory and refuse to allow the enemy to destroy what God has given you. Your battle is personal but so is your God. He is there with you to help you conquer your enemy.

> So be strong and courageous. Do not be afraid and do not panic before them. For the Lord your God will *personally* go ahead of you. He will neither fail you nor abandon you. (Deuteronomy 31:6 NLT)

When the unexpected happens, don't give up. I don't know why, but this reminds me of a recent escapade that I had with sweet potatoes. It seems that on every Thanksgiving without fail, the sweet potatoes and I have a little issue—seriously. I seem to inevitably burn the marshmallows, and then smoke rises from the oven and into the kitchen, sometimes setting off the fire alarm.

My husband likes sweet potatoes one way and one way only. I have tried some amazing recipes using fresh sweet potatoes or mashed sweet potatoes in hollowed-out oranges. But without fail and no matter how fancy I try to make them, he wants the canned sweet potatoes cooked with butter, brown sugar, and cinnamon and then garnished with a thick layer of miniature marshmallows, which are lightly browned but not burnt.

This past Thanksgiving, the sweet potatoes and I had our annual tiff before I could even remove them from the can. As I was using my handheld can opener to open the first of three large cans, the can opener exploded. I'm not kidding. It just came apart, and parts flew all over the cabinet top.

My husband had been standing in the kitchen watching me prepare his favorite dish (He tends to hover when I'm making his favorite dishes). He was amazed at how the can opener had dismantled itself.

Not having another option, I was wondering how I was going to make his sweet potatoes for the big Thanksgiving meal. It was one of the last things that I made before everyone arrived, and it was almost time for the shenanigans to begin.

Not wanting to give up, I asked my husband to go into the garage and to come back with his hammer and chisel. Just minutes later, he came in proudly with a tool in each hand. Together, we pried open the three large cans of his beloved sweet potatoes.

You know me. I can turn almost everything that happens into a life lesson. So as we were prying open the cans, I thought, *We should be that determined to claim and receive our blessings from our Heavenly Father.*

When our unexpected moment occurs, how do we respond? Do we just give up and have a poor-me attitude? Do we take matters into our own hands and work hard to receive the outcome that we desire? Do we turn to the Lord with a humble attitude that is ready to hear His take on the situation and is willingly to learn from it?

It is always our choice. How we handle unexpected moments in life is always up to us. God doesn't push Himself on us. He is a gentleman. He gives us free choice.

Be just as determined to know what God says about your situation as we were in opening the can of sweet potatoes that Thanksgiving. If the can opener breaks, get the hammer and chisel for goodness sakes.

Psalm 56:8 says, "You've kept track of my every toss and turn through the sleepless nights. Each tear entered in Your ledger. Each ache written in Your book" (MSG). Oh I so love this. Only the Lord knows how many times we toss and turn during our sleepless nights. He keeps track of them. Do you wonder why? Because He really, really loves us and desires that we give it all up, lean on Him, trust that He knows what He is doing, and be reassured that His plans are good and not bad. He records our tears like an accountant. Every time we ache, whether it is our bodies or our hearts, He writes it down. Why? Because He loves us.

I loved my babies more than my own life. After I placed them in their cribs at night, I would hover over them for a while, just watching them sleep so innocently and peacefully. When they began to get restless, I would run to their cribs and watch them turn over and sometimes begin to whimper a little. I would lovingly pat them on their tiny backs or rub their little tummies.

When they cried, and their little tears ran down their sweet faces, I would fall apart. I never wanted my precious babies to hurt or to be sad. But even with the amount of love that I had for them—the love that took over my heart—I *never* once wrote down their aches. I *never* once counted and entered their tears into a journal. Oh, how He must love us.

I remember when I was taking care of my mom during the last two weeks of her life. She woke up during the night with excruciating pain, and I prepared her dose of medicine. After I administered it to her, I sat down beside her, held her hand, looked into her eyes, and asked, "Mom, did I learn everything I was supposed to learn from you? Did I listen with my heart and not just my ears?"

She looked at my questioning eyes, as if she had never thought of our relationship that way before. She being the teacher and me being the student, she softly replied, "I don't know."

Those three words left me feeling somewhat empty and helpless because I knew that her journey was nearing an end. There would be no more life lessons to glean from her. She was well on her journey home.

Since then and as a mom, I have tried to give my girls every life lesson that I could, even when they were adamant about not wanting to hear it. I will continue to do so because when God calls me home, I want them to know that I tried my best to teach lessons that would benefit them. The most important one is that Jesus loves them and gave His life for them. The greatest answer to that unselfish act of unconditional love is to love Him back unashamedly and with all they have. In the end, that is the *only* lesson that is going to matter.

As I strive to relay life lessons to them, I pray this prayer (I read it somewhere years ago, and it has stuck with me):

> Dear God, physically show yourself to my children. Speak to them in their dreams; confront them with love during their day and cause their

hearts to desire you. I see them as you see them. They are anointed, redeemed, happy, healthy, and whole, walking out their God-given destiny, surrounded by grace and favor.

It's confession time. Let's take a reality check. Don't judge others, not even in your head. That's one battle you can't win. Here is an example. The other day, I met up with our baby daughter. Her phone was shattered. I looked at the screen and thought, *That's ridiculous. How can one tiny little girl always have broken screens on her phone? She needs to learn how to take care of her property better.* Then my pharisaical attitude said, *I have owned cell phones for many years, and never ever, not even once, has my phone's screen shattered or broken. I take great care of my phones.*

Now, mind you, I did not speak these thoughts out loud. Even though I went with her to the store and helped her replace her phone, I was still thinking these thoughts and replaying them throughout the day, smugly of course, with my self-righteous attitude.

Then it was payback time. Less than twenty-four hours after seeing my daughter's shattered phone, I dropped my cell phone three times. Even though I had a glass protector over the screen, it shattered. You know we are admonished to judge not lest we be judged. I'm telling you not to even judge others in your thoughts. Okay Lord, lesson learned.

My life changed forever on June 28, 1973, and subsequently, I made bad choices that not only affected my life but my future children's lives, grandchildren's lives, and generations to come. Never let anyone tell you that your life doesn't matter and that the choices you make for yourself only affect you. Your life matters. The choices you make matter. Believe me; they will follow you and your bloodline.

I know firsthand that even when life is at its darkest, it will get even darker if you don't turn your heart and life over to the Lord, who loves you. He loves you even in the dark. It has been over forty-seven years since that pivotal day in my life. Today, I still cannot find the good in what happened on that day in 1973. There are still tears and regrets. There is still extreme sadness. But none of these feelings can make anything right or undo what's been done.

This is why I have devoted the rest of my life to being your encourager. You can overcome. I have. You do not have to be a victim. I am not. You can pick yourself up and become that warrior. Accept no defeat. Praise when you don't think there is any reason to.

"*Praise preludes power.*" ~ a Sherryism

Sing when the music has stopped. Singing opens up the soul. Pray when no words come out. Praying is communicating with your creator, and that, my friend, is the secret to victory. You can do this.

Like most of you, I have struggled with the question about bad things happening to God's children. At one point in my life after experiencing more than a few tragic events, I really questioned God. Then I heard this story.

> A young bride lost her handsome husband, just months after they were married. She became somewhat bitter, understandably so. One day her father came to visit her, and she began to talk about her hurt. And how she couldn't understand why God allowed that hurt.
>
> Her wise father replied, "when you were little and you were walking beside me and fell down, I didn't allow

that to happen. It just did. But I was always there to unconditionally pick you up and take care of you, if you allowed me to. I cried when you cried. I was happy when you were happy. That's just like our Heavenly Father."

This was the answer that I had needed to hear all my life. When the bad things happened to me and I fell down and got hurt, I hurt so badly. It was not God's fault. He was not punishing me. He didn't make it happen. It happened. Life happened. But He wanted me to know that He was always right there beside me. He was there to pick me up, to brush away the dirt, to heal the wound, and to hold my hand ... if I only would allow Him to do so. It was many years before I allowed Him to do so.

My friend, if you are experiencing a hurt, take hold of this truth. God didn't do it. In this life, we will experience unimaginable happiness, but eventually and most certainly, there will be times of heart-wrenching sadness, hurt, and what seems like devastation. In these times, please, please remember, God is right there beside you. He will bend down, pick you up, and hold you close. Allow yourself to lean into His arms of love.

Loving and serving God does not mean that

we have a magic wand to wave and life becomes perfect. Life is not perfect. Don't fool yourself into thinking that being a Christian is this magical journey where everything is easy and there are no trials or sadness. That being said, a child of God has a Bible full of promises to claim, hold on to, and help gain the strength and encouragement to get through the tough times.

You don't have to walk your journey without hope. There is hope. There is a way through the trouble and muddle. There is a strong arm to lean upon. There is *Jesus*. He has promised, "I will never leave you nor forsake you" (Deuteronomy 31:8 NKJV), and He has said, "Call upon Me in the day of trouble; I will deliver you" (Psalm 50:15 NKJV). The difference between walking your journey with Jesus and walking your journey without Him is having or not having peace, joy, and love.

Dig into the Word of God. Find your promise. Hold on to it. During our lives' journeys, there are times when it seems like it is *so* hard to keep one foot in front of the other. We can't see what's beyond the bend in the road. When an unexpected landslide is in front of us and winds whip all around us, it's not the time to worry or allow fear to overwhelm us but the time to just fall into God's love. There is no safer place to be. Once we fall into God's love, we don't have to worry about falling out of it. He dispenses armies of angels to watch over us and to go to battle for us.

Do not be discouraged, peeps. You are a child of the one true living God. Jehovah Jireh has got this, regardless of the situation you are in. He is there. Just fall into His love. Go to your prayer room and place your petition before the Lord. Speak faith. Lean on His everlasting arms. Sometimes, when we lean on others, their arms get tired and we become too heavy. That will never happen with the Lord.

"Face uncertainty, not with fear, but with Faith" ~ a Sherryism

Charles Spurgeon, a preacher who lived from 1834–1892, once said, "I have learned to kiss the wave that throws me against the Rock of Ages." I love this. I haven't quite mastered it yet. I am still learning. But I do find comfort in the fact that when that wave tosses me, I fall on the Rock of Ages where I am safe and not destroyed. Thank You, Abba Father.

I have been thinking a lot about how fragile we seem to be. Frankly, I am a little tired of it. I know that because we are imperfect humans, we rely a lot on our feelings. I understand that words either destroy or bring life. I always want to be a life-giver not a life-destroyer. But hear me out. Sometimes, we seem to wear our feelings on our sleeves, and if we get bumped, watch out.

It makes me sad to see so many rifts in relationships and families because of feelings. As children of God, we should be aware of this one thing: Satan will use words to prevent us from doing what God has planned for us. He will cause people to hurt our feelings. Then our minds create storms around the pain. We then put up barriers so that the storms don't do further damage. Now look what has happened. We are in a place we should not be. We are somewhat isolated and feel devastated. We have closed the doors and prevented ourselves from receiving some of the blessings and experiences that God desires for us, all because we consider ourselves fragile.

Stop this stinking thinking today. Let's work on becoming stronger humans and not allow our fragile emotions and minds to always be hurt. We can become stronger. Just as we work out to strengthen our bodies (Well, some of us do—you probably won't see me in the gym), we must work within to become anti-fragile.

"Anti-fragile is power from within." ~ a Sherryism

I once heard this saying: "The Christian who neglects the Holy Spirit is like a lamp that's not plugged in." The person saying this, who is unknown to me, surely was a wise soul. So many times, we forget the third person in the Godhead: the precious Holy Spirit. Jesus said that He would send us a comforter. This comforter is the Holy Spirit. He is such a mighty force, yet we ignore or diminish His power, His presence, and even His existence. I want to know and receive more from my comforter.

Having the Holy Spirit as our guide and comforter enables us to become less fragile. Remember this: We don't have to be perfect.

> God loves using mess-ups who fess up
> and then step up to do mighty works
> for Him.
> —Sharon Jaynes

First Peter 4:10 reads, "Each of you should use whatever gift you have received to serve others as faithful stewards of God's grace in it's various forms" (NIV). Use your gift, even when you are tired, think there is nothing left, and have given, but there is nothing more to give. Stir it up. Ask for the renewing of your spirit, mind, and soul and a fresh anointing. You are special and unique.

You are the only one who owns your gift. Don't hide it. Use it. Become bold. Be that blessing.

At some point in our lives, I think we have all had people that we love seemingly throw us to the wolves. I know I have. Someone I loved once came to my place of employment and told me in front of my coworkers that they were praying I would get killed in a car wreck before I could marry my husband. Thirty years later, I still don't get it. What could I possibly have done to allow this person to think they could be my judge and pray such defeat over my life? That is not love. That is self-righteousness.

Aren't you glad that people don't have the last say over you, no matter who they are? God mends what is broken in you. The words that are spoken over you in hate and ignorance have no power. No matter who throws you to the wolves, grace steps in, and God heals the brokenness.

It doesn't mean you won't have scars because you certainly will. It means you will *not* be devoured. It means your life will be saved. It means you will rise to become a testimony. Grace is not the end, but it is the beginning.

Chapter 3

Seeing It the Biscuit Way

"God does great things through the greatly wounded. God sees the broken as the best and He sees the best in the broken. And He calls the wounded to be the world changers."
—Ann Voskamp

I was recently studying for a message that I wanted to relay to a group of girlfriends during a warrior weekend. During my prayer and study, the Lord spoke to me and said, *Tell the girlfriends that warriors are like biscuits.*

Immediately, I questioned Him. I'm sure I had this incredulous look on my face as I replied,

What? What in the world are you talking about, God? He then gave me this illustration. A biscuit *rises* when it is placed in the fire.

Not many things are better than a hot homemade buttermilk biscuit. Am I right? But guess what? The biscuit that melts in your mouth and gives you so much happiness has gone through the fire for you.

You see, it all started as it was first flipped around and stirred in a bowl. Next, it is slapped onto a cutting board, and it endured some kneading. Then of all things, a rolling pin was brought out and was literally rolled over the biscuit. It went back and forth, not just once, but several times. It took several times to flatten the biscuit into just the right size. Now, if that wasn't enough torture, a round sharp-edged tool cut the biscuit into perfectly round shapes.

The biscuit, thinking it had gone through multiple stages of being stirred, tossed, kneaded, smashed, and cut, was just about to relax on the cutting board when all of a sudden, it was picked up, placed on a piece of cold metal, and then put into a hot oven.

Oh, my goodness. That biscuit, unknowingly and unwillingly (After all, who raises their hand and volunteers to go into the fire?), is placed into the fire. It probably begins to think, *This is it. I'm done, I'm finished. This place I am in is going to destroy me. The heat is too intense. The pan is tanning my backside, for heaven's sake. I'm never going to get out of here. I can't take anymore.* Does this sound familiar?

Then (and this is the part where I begin to cry buckets and praise my Lord and King) just when the biscuit thinks it is over, miraculously, a loving hand reaches into the hot oven and brings that biscuit out of the fire and devastation just in time. When the biscuit is removed from the overwhelming and *almost* consuming heat, it is not ruined, but instead, it is beautiful. It has *risen* to become *exactly* what it was made to be. It does what it was made to do: nourish and bring pleasure to someone.

Warriors, how many times have you been tossed, kneaded, and rolled over (not once, not twice, but a few times)? How many times have you been cut? Then you feel someone pick you up and you think, *Whew. I'm saved. I'm going to be okay.* But immediately, you find yourself in an intense fire and know that you will be destroyed. There is nothing left.

But guess what? Just in time, the Master Chef extends His arm of mercy, lovingly reaches into the inferno of your fire, and pulls you out. He then looks at you and knows, beyond a shadow of a doubt, that you are ready to walk out your destiny and to be the beautiful blessing He knew you would be all along. Whoo hoo!

Warriors, don't be afraid of the fire but *rise* to where God wants you to be.

> **"Rest in the knowledge of the truth that when He sees you have risen to your potential, He will reach out and bring you into your destiny."** ~ **a Sherryism**

Be a biscuit. A biscuit rises when it is placed in the fire.

For over a year, I have been in therapy for a back issue. One day, my doctor, who loves talking to me about my books and ministry, began to talk. He asked me about a new book that I was writing and wondered what the title would be.

I told him, *"Warriors Are Like Pearls and Biscuits."*

He chuckled and said, "Tell me about the biscuit part. I get the pearls, but what does a biscuit have to do with a warrior?"

So I told him about the biscuit, and then (He is so cute. Bless his heart) he said, "Let me play the devil's advocate and ask what happens if the

Master Chef gets busy with something else, He forgets the biscuit, and it burns up?"

I looked him straight in the eye and replied, "The Master Chef will never, never get too busy. The Master Chef will never forget. The Master Chef knows when the exact time comes to bring the biscuit out of the fire. You can count on it."

Rest in knowing that when He sees you have risen to your potential, He will reach out and bring you into your destiny. Praise the Lord today and forevermore.

There is a saying floating around the internet. "A salty Christian makes others thirsty for Jesus, the Water of Life." (Author unknown) I like this. It enlightens me.

For the longest time, I couldn't quite understand the scripture that compared Christians to salt. I could definitely understand the light part. It wasn't hard to see the importance of light showing the way in the darkness. But salt? Well, I knew Jesus said, "You are the salt of the earth. But what good is salt if it has lost its flavor?" (Matthew 5:13 NLT). I understood that salt was used to enhance and to preserve. But I still wasn't sure how I was salt. How was I to live my life as salt?

Then the above quote turned on a light bulb for me. When you taste something salty, you really want to drink water, right? So if I'm walking my journey as a salty Christian, I will make those around me desire to drink of Jesus to quench their thirsts, which will change their lives and their eternities forever. Wow. I got it. Thank You, Lord.

We hear this saying a lot: "Let God ..." Now that is an extremely open-ended statement. Let God what? Well,

Are you tired? Let God give you rest.

Are you discouraged? Let God encourage you.

Are you uncertain? Let God give you clarity.

Are you sad? Let God give you joy.

Are you sick? Let God give you health.

Are you afraid? Let God give you peace.

"Let God." Yes, but as humans, we like to be in control. It is not always easy to let God.

The world teaches us that we can be in control of our own destinies. Be careful, peeps. I do not believe that we are capable of controlling our own destinies in the proper way without Jesus. Why? Because we are mere humans, who are *slightly* informed (no matter how intelligent we are). We see through the glass darkly. In other words, we really don't know zip. Seriously, if we want to live a victorious life, we must let God guide us. We must seek His ways because they are higher than our ways. Then when it comes to the really hard stuff that we face, we must let go and let God." Does this make sense? I hope so. I hope that I have planted a let-God seed in your spirit today.

I'm all about repurposing. I am a junkaholic. I get chills just seeing someone's trash on the side of the curb because I know that I can make it someone else's treasure (and more times than not, my own). I am a bargain hunter. I love the hunt. But I really love scoring the big bargain. You know; the one that almost takes your breath away and makes you run to the counter to pay for it so you can quickly own it.

You know you have done well on your junking trip when you are standing in line at the register and women are circling your buggy (buggy=southern for cart) like sharks while saying "Score," "Wow," and, "Today was your day."

You stand there grinning from ear to ear with joy as you fist-bump, nod your head, and respond, "Oh yeah."

Do you need healing? It's already been proven.

Do you desire to see your family serving the Lord? Oh, that promise is tried and true.

Do you need your finances to increase, multiply, and be restored? That's been tested and proven true as well.

All of God's promises have been thoroughly tested. That is why we love them so much. God cannot and will not fail you. It just won't happen.

Grab your promise and thank God—really tell Him, "Thank You that Your promises are not empty words." Each has been tested and found to be true. It bears repeating: "Your promises have been thoroughly tested that is why I love them so much" (Psalm 119:140 (NLT).

The other day, I was thinking of how we sometimes use the same ingredients and supplies as other people do, yet the outcome can be very different. Here is an example. There are two Subway restaurants in my little community. I love Subway's chopped salads. The people at the restaurant nearest to my home cannot, for the life of themselves, make a chopped salad. Let's just say that it's a tossed salad. But the second restaurant, which is across town (a big whopping mile and a half or two miles), can absolutely make the best chopped salad that I have ever tasted. I will drive the distance to get the best salad.

I always order the exact same ingredients, but the outcome is so totally different at the two restaurants. They use the same type of bowl and the same chopping utensil, but they definitely have a different technique.

Another example is my hairstylist and me. I can purchase her exact products, but I cannot, in any shape or form, style my hair like she does. Here's one more example: My hubby and I love to go to painting classes. The instructor has the identical blank canvases, brushes, and paints that we do. She gives step-by-step instructions as she paints the picture. Her painting is spectacular. Mine and my hubby's look like a two-year-old got into the finger paints.

You know me; I love to turn my daily life into life lessons. So this is what I take away from all these examples: God made us all individuals. Wow. We do not have the same talents, callings, and purposes. He does not need two of me or two of you. He made us all unique.

Even if you desire to follow in someone's footsteps or calling and use the same ingredients or products as that person does, it will not be the same. Why? Because it is not your talent, gift, and calling.

God has given each of us a unique gift that only belongs to us. Work *your* gift. *Be uniquely you.* Your life then becomes *your* masterpiece. It is anointed by God, and it brings Him glory and honor. In turn, you will become a blessing to others like the employees who make the best chopped salad, the hairstylist, or the artistic teacher are.

Sometimes when we are near the end of our workweeks, we are just plain tired. But God reminds us in Galatians 6:9, "So let's not get tired of doing what is good." He continues by saying, "At just the right time" (and not in the time frame we think it should be), "we will reap a harvest of blessing, if we don't give up" (NLT). So let us think about this a minute. We will receive not only a blessing but also a *harvest of blessing.*

When a farmer reaps a harvest, it is not only one ear of corn but an entire cornfield. When a fisherman reaps a harvest, it is not only one fish but an entire boat full.

God says we will reap a harvest of blessing if we don't give up. So, peeps, don't give up, even if you are tired, it's Friday, your feet hurt, your backaches, and your brain is in fog mode. Even if you are experiencing all these things and more, keep doing what is good because at just the right time, you will reap a harvest of blessing. There is no delay in the blessings of God. He is always on time—always.

I once heard a quote: "God is the only one who can show up past the deadline and still be on time" (unknown). Why is this true? Because God doesn't have time lines. He works and lives in a timeless eternity. Only we, who are mere mortals, create deadlines. Putting a deadline on our faith in God and His timing is the most ridiculous human thing we can do. It can pretty much sabotage our faith. God never misses a deadline because He doesn't react to them, period. So stop trying to put Him in a box. There is no box.

Eventually we must learn, believe, and speak in God's timing because His timing is perfect. We have less stress and more peace when we are comfortable knowing God's timing is perfect. Learn to relax while you the wait.

My hubby and I recently planted four rose bushes. They are so beautiful. All four had lots of blooms. But one bush, which was planted at the same time and day and in the same way, was very slow in blooming. While three of the four bushes bloomed the following day, the fourth one did not bloom until the fifth day. Every day, I would go and check it. The buds were very tight. I guess you would call it a late bloomer. But the fact is that when it did bloom, wow, it was every bit as gorgeous and perfect as the other rose bushes.

This little waiting-on-God experience showed me that even when we are in waiting mode and we are getting a little antsy, we must calm down and relax. We do not need to try to rush the perfection of God's timing. Believe me; it will be worth the wait.

> *"When we have pushed back the doubt and our human-based, limited expectations, we have turned the key of faith and unlocked the door for unexpected, unexplainable blessings and divine interventions".* ~ a **Sherryism**

It is easy to say, but to actually live this out is not always as easy. If we are honest with ourselves and our tribe of warriors, we will acknowledge that there are days when focusing on God and not the situation around us is really hard. It is so easy to focus on our circumstances but so lethal as well. It defeats every purpose of our faith.

Let's begin to see our thoughts as the

battlegrounds that they are and then daily present our minds to Jesus as a gift. Let's learn to live by faith and not by sight. I like to say that we live by faith and not by thoughts.

We absolutely have the power to take our negative thoughts to the Lord and to say, "Here, fix these please, and thank You for increasing my faith by replacing them with *Your* thoughts." It takes a faith that you have to dig deep for, but it is worth the dig. It takes asking our warrior tribeswomen to hold our hands up because we do not have the strength to hold them up by ourselves anymore.

It is okay to let our warrior tribe know of our weaknesses. It takes having the knowledge of God's unconditional love and that He is in control. There is absolutely nothing we can do about the situation. We must give it all to Him.

It is worth the effort it takes to refocus: to take our eyes off our circumstance and focus on the Lord because sweet, sweet victory is the greatest feeling on earth. We can look at the ground and see that the giant is dead. Our Giant Killer is alive and well.

I encourage you today, my sweet warrior tribe, no matter what you are facing, lean heavily on the Lord. Focus on Him and not on your circumstances. Build your faith by encircling yourself with your warrior tribe. Your warrior tribe should include praisers and uplifters and not drainers and complainers.

Positivity cannot coexist with negativity. Eventually one will win out, so be a watchman over your soul. Someone once said, "Worrying is like walking around with an umbrella waiting for it to rain" (unknown). Right? What good does worrying do anyway? It just saps your strength.

There are things in life we cannot fix. Only God has that kind of control. So put your umbrella away. It isn't raining. The sun is shining, and the Son is sitting by the right hand of our Father. If the Son and the Father cannot handle the situation, no one can. Should little thoughts of doubt and worry or the torment of what ifs come today, remind yourself who loves you and who fights your battles: the Great I Am and the Giant Killer.

Job 5:9 reads, "He performs wonders that cannot be fathomed, miracles that cannot be counted" (NIV). We have the ability to count to billions, trillions, and beyond. We can even count in light-years. But our God, our Creator, our Provider, our Healer, our Savior, our Way-Maker, our Protector, and our Great I Am performs miracles that cannot be counted. Get you some of that. Stop thinking about gloom and doom. Turn your thoughts toward the God who can and still does. He can do and still does what? Whatever you need Him to do, child of God.

He is not going to let you fall or fail. He is always there to catch you. The Word says that He "commands the Angels to watch over us, lest we dash our foot against a stone" (Psalm 91:11–12 NKJV). Your God doesn't even want you to stumble over rocks, much less fall.

The key is to remember that our timing is not always God's timing. Sometimes we just need to trust Him. Let's be honest, trusting is hard, and we can become anxious about the unknown.

This reminds me that recently I was at one of the malls near me, and I found myself with some extra time between appointments. I decided to just sit, relax, and drink my tea. I found the perfect spot to relax and to people watch.

When I sat down, I noticed a really nice iPhone lying facedown on the chair next to where I was sitting. No one was near the area, and no one had been sitting there when I walked up. So I picked up the phone. Naturally, it was on lock mode, and I couldn't get the owner's information from it. I decided that I would sit there for about thirty minutes, and hopefully, the owner would show up.

When I looked at the locked screen, I saw a picture of a beautiful couple that was dressed elegantly and was attending an event. I liked their faces right away.

Anyway, after sitting there for twenty minutes, guess who showed up? Yep. It was the sweet couple, who looked worried and distressed. They saw someone now sitting in the chair where they had left the phone.

I immediately recognized the woman from the picture on the phone. I smiled my biggest smile and held the phone up to show her that it was safe and in good hands. Oh, my goodness, you will not believe the transformation that relief and joy brought to their faces.

She even grabbed at her heart and exclaimed, "Oh, thank you, thank you. We were so worried."

The man responded, "We got all the way to our car before we noticed we did not have it."

I kept beaming my happiest smile and replied, "I'm so glad you came back. I was going to wait thirty minutes, in the hope that you would return for it. If you did not, I was going to take it to the lost and found area."

The woman offered to buy me a coffee, which I politely turned down. The gentleman said, "How about a trip to Hawaii?" to which I laughingly replied, "Well now, I just might take that."

As they walked away, he looked at me once again with such gratitude, relief, and joy and said,

"I love you." He then turned to his wife, who was smiling, and said, "I do. I love her."

Then they walked away. I continued to sit there a few more minutes, enjoying the feel-good bubble that surrounded me. Now, you know me; I always find the Jesus moment in all of my life experiences. This experience was no different.

As I continued to sit there and to ponder what had just transpired, I realized, *Wow. This is so like us and the Lord. We find ourselves in a predicament and become all stressed and worried. Just like the beautiful couple, we don't know what the outcome will be. We don't realize that the thing we were concerned about—the thing that was completely out of our control— was safe in loving hands.*

All we need to do is seek, and we shall find. They didn't know what they would find when they came back, but I knew. I knew their treasure was safe and secure. Isn't that just like our precious Jesus? On our journey, we make mistakes and sometimes lose our treasures, but when we, as children of God, seek Him and His will, we find out that everything is okay.

We were worried and stressed. Our faith might have been tested. We might have waivered a little bit. But Jesus knew all along that everything was in His hands and was safe and secure. Once we realize this, our joy is restored. We gush, much like the gentleman did, "I love you." Then our faith is increased in the One who holds today and all of our tomorrows.

No matter what we experience, know this: He's got us, and He won't let go of us. We will be okay. Our families will be okay. Every situation will be okay. He smiles upon us with blessings and not curses. Jeremiah 29:11 is my very favorite verse of scripture. It reads, "For I know the plans I have for you declares the Lord; plans to prosper you and not to harm you, plans to give you hope and a future" (NIV).

Stop worrying so much. Take comfort in the fact that as a child of God, you, all your treasures, and your concerns are safe in the hands of your Savior. Praise the Lord today and forevermore.

I was talking to one of my precious girlfriends the other day. She was going through a very hard time, both physically and emotionally. I reminded her, "It's like this: one step at a time, one stone at a time, one giant at a time." That's why we must keep our focus on God and not on our circumstances. That's exactly why we must keep seeing it the biscuit way.

Chapter 4

Why Run When You Can Slay?

"The Spirit of a Warrior resides within you." – Lisa Bevere

I desire the unexplainable miraculous power of God to surround me, engulf me, and overflow out of me, but sometimes, it comes with a battle. In Acts 22, Paul was explaining to the church how Jesus appeared to him when he was walking on the road to Damascus.

Jesus called to him, saying, "Saul, Saul, why are you persecuting me." Paul answered, "Who are you Lord?" Jesus responded, "I am Jesus of Nazareth, whom you are persecuting." Paul then told the church, "And those who were with me indeed saw the light and were afraid, BUT they did not hear the voice of Him who spoke to me" (Acts 22:9 NKJV)

How many times have we *seen* the light of the glory of God, but we did not press in to *hear* what He was saying to us? Why? Are we too busy? Are we too self-absorbed to give the Lord a little bit of our time?

He shows us light, yet there is more. There is His voice. He wants to talk to us too. He so desires that you and I talk to Him. He has lots and lots to say to us. He wants a conversation, peeps. He doesn't just want to shine a light in our direction. How about beginning today? Can we stop long enough to listen for His voice? Wouldn't our world be shaken as we know it, if we stopped long enough to listen for God's voice?

A few years ago, my girls and I took a pottery class. This class went on for several weekends, as there were different stages that we had to learn in making our individual creations. At the first class, we sat down at a potter's wheel. I thought, *Oh wow.* I had heard of the potter's wheel all my life, but sitting down in front of one was a fun and enlightening experience. We were given aprons and a lump of clay. We were shown how to keep the clay moist and then how to dump it—seriously, to just dump it on the middle of the wheel. While stepping on our foot pedals to make the wheels turn, we were shown how to form our clay to a certain height. Then we were told to flatten and then shape it like a container.

We were all doing our own thing and doing well when "Plop." my *entire* creation flew off the potter's wheel. One of my daughters began to laugh at me, and then, "Plop," her creation did the same thing. It was too funny.

The instructor walked over to her and said, "That's what you get for laughing at your mom," and he was right.

Even though this is a funny, special memory, you know I will always find a life lesson. The clay on the potter's wheel is you and me. The potter begins with only a lump of clay, but there is so much potential. He knows it. No one else can see the creation like the Creator can. No one else sees the image like the Creator does. No one else envisions the magnificence of the clay like the Creator does.

"He sees the creation as it is intended to be, because He is the Creator." ~ a Sherryism

Does the clay have any say in how the creator molds and forms it? Nope. The clay is pretty much a useless lump until the potter gets ahold of it. Praise the Lord. Grasp this, peeps. As the clay, we have no say over our destiny. We just need to relax and allow the Potter to work the miracle of His masterpiece.

> *"When my pieces meet the Master, I become His masterpiece."* ~ a Sherryism

We hear a lot about DNA these days. But the only DNA that matters is His. Are we a child of God with His DNA running through our veins? If so, we walk in victory. There is no surrender to the enemy. We are not POWs or MIAs. There is no defeat. We have inherited the power and the might of the Great I Am. We share the same blood as His Son, Jesus. Come on, warriors. Renew your spirit today and grab hold of this miracle. Our DNA is forever changed when we accept Jesus as our Lord and Savior. Whoo hoo!

> *"As a child of God, there is nothing but Victory in our DNA."* ~ a Sherryism

With your head held high, shield in place, weapon drawn, you are a warrior. Embrace it. Get excited about it. You do not have to live defeated and downtrodden.

Someone, unknown to me, once said, "Understand your worth. Value your life. Appreciate your blessings." I believe that when we appreciate our blessings—no matter how small they are—our attitudes change. When we value our lives, we value others. When we understand our worth, we get a glimpse of the person that God wants us to be. Become comfortable with who you are. You should never compare yourself to anyone else. You need to know that God made you to shine for Him.

There's one more thing. God's promises for us are unshakeable and unstoppable. Whatever He has promised you, it will happen. When the enemy brings up all your mistakes and shortcomings, look him in the eye and say, "Those things don't matter to God because He doesn't see them anymore. They are all under the blood of Jesus." Remind the enemy that God has promised you good things, which will come to pass because God said they would.

It has nothing to do with what you or I have done in the past. It has nothing to do with who we are, except for the fact that we belong to God and that we receive His promises, which are what? They are unshakeable and unstoppable. So claim your promises with bold faith. Your Heavenly Father is a bold God.

Psalm 119:50 reads, "Your promise revives me; it comforts me in all my troubles" (NLT). Do you read and understand your Bible enough to know God's promises for you? A good excuse the enemy loves to hear us say is, "The Bible is too hard to understand." When we feel this way, we should shake up our devotions. Use different translations. I use KJV, NKJV, NLT, and MSG translations of the Bible. Compare verses in each one. Use study plans and devotionals.

Ask God to give you the knowledge and understanding of His Word. Ask Him to enlighten your heart and to bring His thoughts into your mind. Then practice putting those thoughts front and center as you walk out your day. The more you do this, the more you are set up for a closer and clearer relationship with the Author. You will begin to grasp the enormity of the promises that He has made.

Never doubt the impact that you have on others. You are a warrior who has been chosen by God and empowered with whatever it takes to bring victory to yourself and to other warriors. Release the spirit of a warrior within you and be that blessing to others today.

I like this quote, "Speak the truth, even if your

voice shakes" (unknown). It reminds me that even when I'm feeling inadequate, I am still a warrior. Even if my voice shakes, I will still speak the truth.

I am and always have been an introvert. While growing up, I had zero confidence. Circumstances that occurred in my late teenage years and early twenties clouded my view of my self-worth even more. There were times when I could not even hold my head up. So why on earth would God want to use me? I have no clue. But hey, He has been known to use a donkey (wink, wink).

As I have grown older, I still find myself battling boldness. I looked up the definition of the word *bold*, and it said that it meant courageous and confident.

Joshua 1:9 reads, "Have I not commanded you? Be strong and courageous. Do not be afraid; do not be discouraged, for the Lord your God will be with you wherever you go" (NIV). We should always be bold, courageous, and confident, not in our own selves but in the One who resides inside of our hearts. We should speak to our hearts and say, "Heart be bold." We should speak to our spirits, saying, "Spirit be bold."

As children of God, we of all people should let our voices be heard. Pray for boldness and that your life will radiate God's power. Be bold. Be confident. Be courageous. That is what He desires for us. God wants us to live securely in the knowledge of who we are because we belong to Him. There is nothing He cannot do.

Sometimes we battle feelings of displacement as we grow older. For instance, when I was in my twenties, I fought every day just to keep my head above water and to be the lone provider for my two little girls. In my thirties, I battled an abusive marriage, which eventually ended in a very messy divorce.

In my forties, life rocked. I was on top of the world. Life was good. I married the love of my life. My children were growing older. I was blessed with my grandbabies. I had an amazing job. I worked with awesome people and raised funds for local hospitals and hospice houses.

In my fifties, I ventured to own my own business, which was a highly successful tearoom and antique boutique. Life was perfect. Eventually, I moved to Oklahoma and met many forever friends, whom I still adore.

But my sixties, wow, they have been a challenge. Even though I'm still blessed with my truly amazing husband, my children, and grandchildren (who are all grown and live close by), I have, at times, felt very alone and displaced. I have allowed the enemy to overwhelm me with petty, immature emotions. There are times when

I have allowed what I thought was happiness depend on whether my children were happy or not.

Seriously? Are you kidding me? Here's a newsflash: My children's happiness is solely dependent upon them and how they respond and react to what life throws at them. Neither their happiness nor mine is based on me protecting and providing for them or even agreeing with their life choices.

My happiness is solely dependent on me. As I write this chapter of my life, I choose the happiness that can only come from Jesus Christ, my Lord and Savior because when I choose Him, everything else falls into place.

Our needs, concerns, situations, and prayers are all the same size in the eyes of God.

> *"There is nothing too small for God to minimize, and there is nothing too large for Him to become overwhelmed by."* ~ a **Sherryism**

God, who can speak this world into existence by His voice, can surely take care of anything, whatever the size, that life throws at us.

I woke up a few days ago thinking of tornados. They play havoc. The state of Oklahoma is right in what scientists and weather experts call Tornado Alley. Each year, hundreds of tornados dance all over the state.

I resided for more than a decade in Anadarko, Oklahoma (home of Indian City, USA). The Native Americans believed a tornado would never hit Anadarko directly because the Washita River runs through this small town. Many times, the tornado sirens went off, warning residents to take shelter, but the little town always survived.

When I think about it, I realize that our lives are much like the little community of Anadarko. Life's storms play havoc with us, both physically and emotionally. There may be times when you feel as though you are residing in Tornado Alley. But if we have the River of Life (Jesus) running through our very core, we are protected from devastation. Oh, child of God, you have protection. He has seen to it.

> *"The tornados of your life will not destroy you when the River of Life runs through you"* ~ a **Sherryism.**

We sometimes wonder why life becomes so hard. As I have grown older (and I hope a little wiser), I have learned this secret: It is very easy to get caught up in the pressures and demands that people, society, a job, a family, and just life in general can place upon us. But when the Lord asks to be first priority in our lives and we make Him our first priority, life can become less stressful and more enjoyable.

If I think I'm too busy in the morning to have my prayer time and talk with Jesus, I find I become bombarded with stress. If I don't pray and seek His direction over every decision I make, I find that I make hasty decisions that lead me to places where I should never go. When I don't give Him first place in my life, well, that is just a disaster waiting to happen. This is not just for me. We have all been made to worship. We will worship something or someone.

I want to encourage you today to try this little experiment for just one week: Give God the first part of your day, allow Him to be the priority in every decision that you make, and give Him first place in your life. Then see what happens. Someone once told me, "We rise, we pray, we slay in Jesus name."

Warriors, I want to take a moment to share something with you, which has become a strength in my journey. In Luke 22, Jesus presents communion to His disciples. Throughout the New Testament, we are encouraged to do this in remembrance of the sacrifice that Jesus made for our healing and salvation.

For years, I had always relied on my pastor and church to administer communion to me. But a few months ago, I encountered a physical and emotional issue. God impressed upon me to begin to take communion in my home. It would be just me and Jesus, privately and one on one. I had some leftover fast-food crackers in my pantry. I bought a six-pack of small bottles of grape juice. I broke off small pieces of a cracker and took one small drink of juice every day. I read different scriptures about communion.

At first, I felt a little weird because it was just me alone taking my communion. But each day, I began to see a change in me. I began to feel closer to Jesus, and His sacrifice became very personal to me. I began to feel His compassion for me. My body and spirit began to heal. I am telling you that I take my personal communion with just me and Jesus all the time now every day. I encourage you warriors and believers that if you want to change your relationship with your Savior, this is a good place to start.

We are planners. We plan for everything. We plan for what we will wear. We plan for what we will cook. We plan for our weekend adventures. We plan our vacations. We plan surprises for friends and family. We plan for holidays. We plan at our jobs. We just love to plan. We like to feel like we're in charge. We absolutely love when our plan comes together.

Yet, we have a Heavenly Father who has a totally out-of-this-world (seriously and in every sense of the word) plan for us, and we have trouble trusting His plan. Why in the world would we think that we, as mere silly humans, could even envision the dream that God the Father and the Creator has for us? Let's grab hold of Jeremiah 29:11 (NLT) "For I know the plans I have for you, says the Lord. They are plans for good and not for disaster, to give you a future and a hope." Then after we grab hold, let's give every situation that is crowding our space back to the Lord. Let's allow His peace to flow over us. Let's believe and trust that His plan—whatever it is, even though we may not see or understand it—will be and is phenomenal.

My siblings and I performed in our family's gospel group. We sang a song "I've Got Confidence". It went like this, "I've got confidence. My God is gonna see me through. No matter what the case may be. I know He's gonna fix it for me."

Faith is being determined like Job was in the Bible. He said, "Though God slay me, yet I will trust Him." You can wish upon a star, you can throw a coin into a fountain, and you can pull off a turkey wishbone. None of these things will cause God to stop and take notice. But when we exercise our faith in Him (even if it is just the size of the smallest mustard seed), He stops. He sees. He hears. He reacts. Our faith reaches the throne, and He makes a way when there is absolutely no way.

God is God. He never changes. He is the same God who parted the Red Sea. The ground wasn't even damp. He is the same God who made a donkey talk and spoke from a bush that was on fire. He is the same God.

> **"Whatever you are facing, exercise your faith and increase your confidence in His faithfulness." ~ a Sherryism**

Each of us has prayers that we want answered. Our issues may be extreme, and the outcomes may be completely out of our human control. Fear takes on a life of its own, but if we can take hold of faith in our God, the Great I Am, fear has to tuck its tail and run. Why? As the words of the song "My God Is So Big" say, " My God is so big and so strong and so mighty, there's nothing My God cannot do." We must learn to walk in faith.

First Corinthians 2:5 reads, "That your faith should not stand in the wisdom of men, but in the power of God" (KJV). Faith in man is hit and miss at best. Faith in man is limited, sometimes powerless, a waste of time, and disappointing. Instead of having faith in the *creation*, let us set our faith in the *Creator*, wherein lies *power* unlimited, *manifestation* of miracles, and *victory*. Let's adjust the focus of our faith.

Faith doesn't need sense. In fact, our human common sense can actually delay our faith. It can convince us that faith isn't necessary, isn't reality, is make-believe, and is ridiculous. Common sense says that there is no way the experience you are having is faith.

But God (I love God's buts) says,

1. It is impossible to please God without faith. (Hebrews 11:6 NLT)
2. If you have faith, even as small as a mustard seed, you can say to a mountain, "Move from here to there," and it will move. (Matthew 17:20 NLT)
3. Faith is the substance of things hoped for and the evidence of things not seen. (Hebrews 11:1 NKJV)

4. You can pray for anything, and if you have faith, you will receive it. (Matthew 21:22 NLT)

5. Your faith should not be in the wisdom of men but in the power of God. (1 Corinthians 2:5 NKJV)

These are just a few nuggets that are found in scripture regarding what God says about faith. Let us leave the ego and the common sense behind as far as our faith is concerned. When we do, I believe we will be pleasantly surprised to see how things turn around.

God means business. Do we? I once heard this quote, "Your faith can move mountains and your doubt can create them" (author unknown).

Choose faith over doubt. Choose faith over fear. Choose victory over defeat. Choose triumph over tragedy. Choose health over sickness. Choose hope over despair. Choose love over hate. Choose faith.

"Choose the mustard seed of faith over the seed of doubt and fear." ~ a Sherryism

Faith banishes fear. The word *fear* is powerful. To those who don't know Jesus (and to some who do), the word *fear* probably seems more powerful than the word *faith*. But it isn't so. There are two ways to look at fear. I once heard it explained like this: "When it raises its ugly head, we can '<u>F</u>orget <u>E</u>verything <u>A</u>nd <u>R</u>un' or we can '<u>F</u>ace <u>E</u>verything <u>A</u>nd <u>R</u>ise.'" Which one do you choose?

> The God of peace will soon crush satan under your feet. (Romans 16:20 NLT)

This verse in the Message translation reads, "Stay alert like this, and before you know it the God of peace will come down on satan with both feet, stomping him into the dirt." I love, love, love this translation. I can just see God stomping Satan into the dirt.

We limit God with our fears when all He desires is for us to believe with faith that He can do exactly what He says He can do. Someone once said, "God's word in your heart equals God's power in your life" (unknown). I love this quote.

Sometimes it can be difficult to make studying God's Word a priority. The enemy of our soul realizes that if he can continually keep us away from knowing God's Word, he has stripped us of knowledge. When we are stripped of knowledge, we are not aware of the enormous power that God promises and freely gives to us. We cannot claim promises we don't know about. Begin to read the Word of God. Increase your knowledge. Increase your power.

People are always discussing what Jesus would have looked like when He lived on earth and what He looks like now. It really doesn't matter to me what my Lord looks like. He is all things to all people. When we look upon His face, we will be engulfed in His eyes. They will be endless pools of love and peace. We will feel His heart of compassion and will probably fall on our knees in the purest form of worship we have ever known.

What does He look like? He looks like nothing and no one we have ever seen before or will ever see again. He looks like unconditional, unending love. That is what He looks like.

I believe that when faith becomes the norm in our lives, God enters the room. Let's look at a few examples of what happens when God enters the room.

Daniel in the Den of Lions

In Daniel 6, we find the story of Daniel. The short version of the story is that Daniel was thrown into a den of lions because he prayed to God and not to the king. The king, King Darius had been tricked into signing a decree stating anyone not praying to him would be thrown into a den of lions. When he found out that Daniel (who was his friend) had been arrested for praying to God, the king was very upset with himself for making the decree.

As the men were coming to place Daniel in the den of lions, the king told Daniel, "Your God, will deliver you." Then he went home, fasted, and stayed awake all night.

Very early on the next day, the king went to the den of lions. He called out to Daniel. By the way, calling out to Daniel was definitely an act of faith because by all human standards, the hungry lions should have torn Daniel apart and feasted upon him. Daniel should have been dead.

Daniel answered, "I'm okay oh king. My God sent His angel and shut the mouths of the lions and they did not hurt me." *God entered the room.*

Shadrach, Meshach, and Abed-Nego

In Daniel 3, we see the story of the three Hebrew men, Shadrach, Meshach, and Abed-Nego. Again, the short version of the story is that King Nebuchadnezzar built a golden image. He decreed that everyone must bow down to this image and worship it.

The three Hebrew men did not and would

not. Word about it reached the king, and he was mad. He commanded them to be placed in a fiery furnace. He had the furnace heated up seven times hotter than usual. Because the furnace was so hot, it killed the men who placed Shadrach, Meshach, and Abed-Nego into it. But the fire did not touch the Hebrew men.

When the king looked into the furnace, he said, "Didn't we put three bound men into the fire? I see four men and they are all walking around, not bound, not hurt and the fourth is like the Son of God." He then commanded them to come out of the fiery furnace.

The fire had had no power over them. Their hair had not even been singed, and their garments did not even smell like smoke. *God entered the room.*

The Centurion's House

In Luke 7, we find the story of the centurion and his servant. The short version of the story is that Jesus was traveling near Capernaum. When he entered the city, a centurion sent elders of the town to approach Jesus and to ask him to come to his home because one of his favorite servants was very sick and ready to die. So Jesus went with the elders.

Jesus wasn't very far from the house when some of the centurion's friends told him that the centurion did not feel worthy for Jesus to come to his house. The centurion had said that if Jesus would just say the word, he knew that his servant would be healed (another act of faith).

When the elders arrived back at the centurion's house, they found that the servant was indeed healed. *God entered the room.*

Lazarus

In John 11, we see the story of Lazarus. Again, the short version is that Jesus had a friend whom He really loved named Lazarus. Lazarus became sick, and before Jesus could get to him, Lazarus died.

When Jesus finally got there, he found out that Lazarus had already been in the grave for four days. Lazarus's family members were brokenhearted, and they blamed Jesus for not getting there sooner (Wow, does blaming Jesus for not getting to us sooner sound familiar?). They did say that they still believed (there is that faith again) that whatever Jesus asked God to do, God would do it.

When Jesus got to Lazarus's grave, scripture says that Jesus cried. He then told some of the people who were there to remove the stone from the front of the tomb. He said, "Lazarus, come forth." Then Lazarus came out of the tomb, but his hands and feet were still bound with funeral cloths.

I get such a visual from this. I picture Lazarus hopping out of the grave, like a bunny hop, because his feet and hands were still bound. Jesus told the people to loosen Lazarus's funeral bindings and to let him go. Lazarus was alive. *God entered the room.*

I have just given you four examples, two from the Old Testament and two from the New Testament, of God's power when He enters a room. There are so many more examples in the Bible, as well as modern-day experiences, of how, when *God enters the room* and faith is alive, unexplainable miracles happen. Set yourself in a position for increased faith so that you can receive your miracle when *Jesus enters your room.* Whoo hoo!

Chapter 5

What Is a Warrior?

"Every warrior is different, even if that warrior has the same instructor."
~ a Sherryism

What does it take to become a warrior? First and foremost, we must know who our Commander is and what we are fighting for. So let's look at this scripture:

> I pray that from His glorious, unlimited resources He will **empower me with inner strength** through His Spirit. Then Christ will make His **home in my heart** as I trust in Him. **My roots will grow down**

into God's love and keep me strong. And may I have the **power to understand**, as all God's people should, **how wide, how long, how high** and **how deep** His love is. May I experience **the love of Christ**, though it is **too great** to understand fully. Then I will be **made complete** with all the **fullness of life and power** that comes from God. Now all glory to God, **who is able**, through His **mighty power** at **work within me** to **accomplish infinitely more** than I might ask or think. Glory to Him in the church and in Christ Jesus through all generations forever and ever. Amen. (Ephesians 3:16–30 NLT)

Know your commander. In Matthew 16:15, Jesus asked his disciples (who were his band of warriors), "Who do you say I am?" (NIV). In Matthew 16:16, one of the disciples, Peter, answered, "You are the Messiah, the Son of the living God" (NIV).

Many names refer to the Lord in the Bible. Some are:

Jehovah Jireh: Our Provider
Jehovah Rophe: Our Healer
Jehovah Shalom: Our Peace
Jehovah Yaweh: Our Salvation
Jehovah Nissi: Our Battle Fighter

The Bible gives us many attributes, names, and descriptions of the Lord. It would take me forever, I believe, to talk about our Commander in Chief, but allow me to name a few in the New King James Version:

He is your Commander/Leader (Isaiah 55:4)
He is your Lawyer/Advocate (1 John 2:1)
He is your Counselor (Isaiah 9:6)
He is your Mediator (1 Timothy 2:5)
He is your Deliverer (Romans 11:26)
He is your Guide (Psalm 48:14)
He is your Redeemer (Isaiah 54:5)
He is your King (Zechariah 9:9)
He is your Lawgiver/Judge (Isaiah 33:22)
He is your Healer (Isaiah 53:5)
He is your Savior (Luke 2:11)
He is your Shield/Stronghold/Refuge (Genesis 15:1 and 2 Samuel 22:3–4)
He is your Teacher/Lord (John 13:13)

But my very favorite descriptions/names of God are:

I am who I Am **(**Exodus 3:14)
I Am (John 8:58)

Believing my Commander is I Am Who I Am and He is the Great I am assures me that He will absolutely lead me to victory in every battle that I face.

While recently having a conversation with the Lord, I heard Him whisper into my heart, *Who am I to you?*

I answered, *Why Lord, You are the Great I am* (Because that's my favorite thing to call Him).

I heard it a second time: *Who am I to you?*

I automatically said, *You are the Alpha and Omega. The beginning and the end* (Because that pretty much sums up everything, right?).

Then I heard it a third time: *Who am I to you?*

Then I replied, *I get it now, Lord.* With tears flowing down my cheeks, I answered, *You are my everything. You are my burden-bearer, my way-maker, my light in the dark, my pain-taker, my hope-carrier, my chain-breaker, and my sin-deliverer. You are the reason I wake up every morning, my life-giver. You are with me when I close my eyes at night, my peace-giver. Yes, Lord, You are my everything."*

When you are living every day in fellowship with the Lord, you position yourself in a place of continuous victory. When the enemy brings battle to you, you don't go out looking for the victory, but *you bring the victory to the battle.* How? It's simple. When you are in fellowship with the Great I Am, you are in a constant victory mode. You are never without it.

Your enemy knows this, and he tries to convince you that you *do not have* victory, that you *never had* victory, and that you *will never have* victory. Yet all the time he knows that you do. He knows it is already a done deal. If we could only grasp and keep our minds set on this level of victory acknowledgement, what couldn't we accomplish? It's not a victory that is ahead of us but a victory that is *now.* Whoo hoo!

> The Lord God is my strength and my song He has given me victory. (Isaiah 12:2 NLT)

He spoke, and our world came into existence. Sometimes I just have to shake my head at people. Scientists and astronomers make me laugh. For example, when I was growing up, we were taught that there were nine planets and that the one farthest away was named Pluto.

Now in the last few years, scientists and astronomers have decided that Pluto is not really a planet. So they removed it from the list of known planets. It was dethroned. It lost its membership in the planet club. Bummer, dude. I read just last week that they think the ninth planet might be a huge black hole or a black circle. Really? What does this even mean?

What about Saturn? We were taught that Saturn had beautiful rings around it. Now scientists and astronomers are saying that the rings are disappearing. The very things that made Saturn unique—the beautiful rings protecting and supporting it in orbit—are now vanishing?

Sometimes, I think, *Now just wait a minute. Who are these scientists and astronomers? What telescopes and computers are they using? Why do we believe them? After all, no matter how much more intelligent or knowledgeable they are, they are still just like me and you—mere mortals. But the God who created the heavens, all that they hold, the earth, and all that is in it is still the same. He is the Great I Am.*

Okay, now that we have learned about our Commander, let's talk about us as warriors.

According to the Merriam-Webster dictionary, the definition of a warrior is "a person who is known for being involved in warfare; someone who is engaged in some struggle or conflict." Once, I read that a warrior protects everything she holds dear—her family, her country, and her faith—and she stands up to *whatever threatens it* and proclaims, "You will not hurt what I hold dear. You will not hurt what I love without first coming through me." A warrior stands in the gap. She becomes the hedge.

So what does it mean to be a warrior? What must we do to become victorious warriors? I emphasize the word *victorious*. Why? Because there are a lot of warriors out there, right? Not every warrior who is in a battle is a victor. Am I right? In every battle, someone has to lose, *but it is not you.* Every child of God is a victorious warrior. Believe it. Claim it. Stand upon it. Never, ever doubt it.

If we want to become victorious warriors, there are a few things we need to learn and practice daily.

1. Warriors know their enemy.
2. Warriors know their armor.
3. Warriors are skillful, well trained, and knowledgeable.

4. Warriors are equipped.
5. Warriors fight side by side and shoulder to shoulder.
6. Warriors are relentless, fierce, and determined.
7. Warriors are courageous.
8. Warriors are bold.
9. Warriors sparkle (Of course, you know I had to put this one in, but it's true).

1. Warriors Know Their Enemy

Jesus said in John 10:10, "The thief does not come except to steal, and to kill, and to destroy" (NKJV). First Peter 5:8 reads, "Be alert and of sober mind. Your enemy the devil prowls around like a roaring lion looking for someone to devour" (NIV).

Know your enemy. He is the destroyer of your soul. He likes to see you in turmoil, confused, and tormented. He likes to see you anxious and fearful. He loves to see you worry about everything. Peter reminds us that our enemy wants to devour us in any way that he can. Know that he is sly. He is clever. He cannot tell the truth. Be alert. Be aware. Be proactive in how you fight the battle he tries to engage you in.

2. Warriors Know Their Armor

The Bible very clearly paints a picture of and explains our armor. Ephesians 6:13–17 reads,

> Therefore, put on <u>every piece of God's armor</u>, so you will be able to resist the enemy in the time of evil. Then <u>after the battle</u>, you will <u>still be standing firm</u>. Stand your ground, putting on the **belt of truth**, and the **body armor of God's righteousness**. For **shoes**, put on the **peace that comes from the Good News** so that you will be <u>fully prepared</u>. In addition, to all of these, hold up the **shield of faith**, to stop the fiery arrows of the devil. Put on **salvation, as your helmet**, and the **sword of the Spirit**, which is the **word of God**. (NLT)

So our warrior armor includes

> A belt—truth
> Body armor—God's righteousness
> Shoes—peace
> A shield—faith
> A helmet—salvation
> A sword—the Word of God

It looks as though God has us *completely covered* so that we are able to come out of the battle as victors.

3. Warriors Are Skillful, Well-Trained, and Knowledgeable

We learn skills, right? We are not born with any life skills. At birth, we do not possess the skill of changing our clothes or feeding ourselves. When we come into this world, we don't even know that we can hold things in our hands, and we suck on our toes—seriously. Every one of my babies found their tiny little toes and sucked on them. I'm sure we all did it. I'd like to see us try it now though. (wink wink) Through training, we mastered the skill of crawling, then walking, then feeding ourselves, and then changing our clothes.

As a warrior, we must continue to train, study, and learn. Second Timothy 2:15 reads, "Study to show thyself approved unto God, a workman [and I like to say a warrior] that needeth not to be ashamed, rightly dividing the word of truth" (KJV). God wants us to always hone our skill of knowing what the Word of God says. He wants us to always be on our guard so that we can protect our hearts and minds, and we will not be led astray by the enemy of our souls.

The enemy of your soul knows the Word of God. He can quote it to you. He quoted it to Jesus. That was pretty bold. Jesus answered the enemy with scripture. He knows the importance of studying, training, and acquiring knowledge. We *must* remember and practice what God says about us, our families, our circumstances, our health, and our nation.

4. Warriors Are Equipped

Warriors are equipped with the weapons of warfare. Second Corinthians 10:4 reads, "The weapons we fight with are not the weapons of the world. On the contrary, they **have divine power to demolish strongholds**." (NIV). Wait a minute. Did you hear that? Let's read it again: "The weapons we fight with are not the weapons of the world. On the contrary, they **have divine power to demolish strongholds**."

So what are these warrior weapons? The warrior weapons of spiritual warfare include the following.

Prayer

Prayer changes things. It is the key to communicating with our Commander. Ephesians 6:18 reads, "Praying always with all prayer and supplication in the Spirit" (KJV).

Praise and Worship

When we sing and praise, the Lord sets up ambushes against our enemies. Second Chronicles 20:22 reads, "Now when they began to sing and praise – the Lord set up ambushes against the people of Ammon, Moab, and Mount Seir, who had come against Judah and they were defeated" (NKJV).

> *"Counting our blessings decreases our tendency to worry."* ~ a Sherryism

Counting our blessings every day and living in a state of thankfulness and praise keeps us focused on all the good things God has done and is doing in our lives. They build our faith to become better warriors.

The Name of Jesus

Jesus's name is above all other names. There is incredible power in the name of Jesus. Every knee will bow before Him.

Philippians 2:9–11 reads, "Therefore, God elevated Him to the <u>place of highest honor and gave Him the name above all</u> <u>other names</u>, that at the name of Jesus every knee should bow, in heaven and on earth and under the earth and every tongue declare that Jesus Christ is Lord, to the glory of God the Father" (NLT). Remember that the name of Jesus is the most powerful of all your warrior weapons.

Fasting

Fasting is essentially giving up food (or something else you love, such as TV, sports, reading, etc.) for a period of time, in order to focus your thoughts on God. During a fast, we warriors read our Bibles, pray, and worship.

As an example, in Psalm 35:13, David remarked, "I humbled myself with fasting" (NKJV). Jesus himself was an example for us. Matthew 4:1–2 reads, "Then Jesus was led up by the Spirit into the wilderness to be tempted by the devil. And when He had fasted forty days and forty nights, afterward He was hungry" (NKJV). In Matthew 17:21, we learn that there are certain prayers that are not answered except when we add fasting to our prayer petitions.

Fasting is a very personal weapon of warfare, but it can bring the greatest results. No two methods of fasting are alike for any warrior, and no two fasts are usually alike. What you fast and the length of your fast are just as personal as your walk with the Lord.

Your Testimony

Revelation 12:11 reads, "And they have defeated him by the blood of the Lamb and by their testimony." (NLT). We know that firsthand testimony is highly respected. In a court of law, a person's testimony can make or break a case.

Our enemy can come against us with everything he's got. But when we've had an experience and a personal encounter with Jesus and we now have a testimony, we don't have to argue with anyone, especially our enemy. We have had a firsthand encounter, and we believe. Remember, it's *your* testimony, and it is powerful.

> **"The more we realize how blessed we are, the more the giants in our vision become less intimidating."** ~ a Sherryism

I grew up in a Pentecostal church. Wednesday night services were a little more laid back than the structured Sunday services were. One part that I look back on is the testimony time. This was when anyone could stand up and tell how the Lord had answered prayer during that week or just stand up and say, "I love the Lord," (which was what a lot of us young people did). It was simple, there was no pressure, and it was always on a volunteer basis. Some nights, there were a lot of testimonies. Other nights, there were just a few.

I always wondered why this sweet intimate time was included. What was the purpose? Did anyone really care what anyone had to say? Then I realized the answer after reading Revelation 12:11. It reads "And they defeated him by the blood of the Lamb, and by their testimony" (NLT). Warriors, we win our battles by the word of our testimonies. Whether it is through singing a song or speaking to a friend or a crowd, never be ashamed to spread your testimony. It is your victory seed. Spread it. Water it.

5. Warriors Fight Side By Side and Shoulder to Shoulder

In Matthew 18:20, Jesus spoke these words, "For where two or three gather in my name, there am I with them" (NIV). The Lord knows that it is easier to be defeated when we fight our battles alone. That is exactly why He places other girlfriends and warriors in our lives.

My bestie, Tari Nixon, and I have been friends for over half our lifetimes. We have decided that we cannot go through our low spots at the same time. I'm being honest here and realizing that we all have our low spots from time to time. That's life here on this planet.

When I need a word of encouragement and a lift in my spirit, Tari always comes through with words that I need to hear to help me receive my victory. When she is in her own low spot, I am always, always there to encourage and to push her on to receive all the good things that God has planned for her and to receive her victory.

We fight side by side, not only to have each other's backs but also to bring each other strength and to help carry each other's burdens. As warriors, we must band together with other warriors. There is strength in numbers.

6. Warriors Are Relentless, Fierce, and Determined

Hebrews 10:39 reads, "But we do not belong to those who shrink back and are destroyed, but of those who have faith and are saved" (NIV). First Corinthians 15:58 reads, "Therefore, my beloved brothers and sisters, stand firm. Let nothing move you" (NIV).

You were made to stand tall. You were not made to be wishy washy. You were made to be relentless, fierce, and determined. It takes all three to be a victorious warrior.

7. Warriors Are Courageous

First Chronicles 28:20 reads, "Be strong and courageous and do the work. Do not be afraid or discouraged, for the Lord God, my God is with you. He will not fail you or forsake you" (NIV). Psalm 27:1 declares, "The Lord is my light and my salvation, so why should I be afraid?" (NLT). First Corinthians 16:13 reads, "Be on guard. Stand firm in the faith. Be courageous. Be strong" (NLT).

God commands us to have courage, and that means having faith and confidence in Him. By learning scripture, we can find the courage God desires for us. In order to have *courage*, we must have *faith* and *believe*. These three go hand in hand.

In Mark 5:36, Jesus says, "Don't be afraid, just have faith" (NLT). Have courage, warrior.

8. Warriors Are Bold

Proverbs 28:1 reads, "The wicked run away when no one is chasing them, but the godly are as BOLD as lions" (NLT). Psalm 138:3 reads, "In the day when I cried out, You answered me, and made me BOLD with strength in my soul" (NKJV).

Acts 4:39 reads, "Now Lord, consider their threats and enable your servants to speak your word with great BOLDNESS" (NIV). Acts 4:13 reads,

> The members of the council were amazed when they saw the BOLDNESS of Peter and John, for they could see that they were ORDINARY men with NO SPECIAL training in the scriptures. They also recognized them as men who HAD BEEN WITH JESUS. (NLT)

You don't have to hold a degree in theology for God to use you and to give you boldness. This scripture holds the key: They were not scholars, they had no special training, *but they had been with Jesus.* When you are bold, you know that God is always on your side, so there is never a reason to fear.

I once read a quote by Edwin Louis Cole, author and founder of the Christian Men's Network. He said, "Prayer in private results in **boldness** in public." Evangelist Dwight L. Moody once said, "When we find a man meditating on the words of God, my friends, that man is full of **boldness** and is **successful**."

9. Warriors Sparkle

You were made to be a warrior princess. You were made to sparkle.

According to the Merriam-Webster Dictionary, *sparkle* means, "To throw out sparks; to perform brilliantly; to give off or reflect bright moving points of light." Dictionary.com defines *sparkle* this way: "to shine or glisten with little gleams of light, as a brilliant gem; glitter; coruscate; a sparkling appearance, luster, play of light." Vocabulary.com explains *sparkle* as the following: "to shine with a bright, glistening shimmering light."

Sparkle can also refer to joy or merriment. When you are having a really good time, your face will sparkle. As a verb, *sparkle* means to be lively and excited or so brilliant at something that you shine above the rest.

"Allow the <u>spark</u> in your <u>sparkle</u> to ignite a fire." ~ a Sherryism

Zechariah 9:16 reads, "The Lord their God, will save His people on that day as a shepherd saves his flock. They will SPARKLE in His land like jewels in a crown" (NIV). Psalm 34:5 reads, "Those who look to Him for help will be radiant with JOY" (NLT). In Mathew 5:16, Jesus says, "Let your light shine before others" (NIV).

Many people have wandered into the darkness while on their journeys. With your tiniest spark, you can absolutely shine light upon their paths. Have you ever turned off every light in your home and then found that the light from your VCR or coffee pot display shines enough light for you to walk through that room? We take these tiny lights for granted until darkness shrouds the room. Then we are thankful for their lights, no matter their sizes.

As children of God, that's the way we are supposed to shine in an otherwise darkened world. Our light may look insignificant in the daylight, but it shines brightly in the night to those who need it. Never, ever doubt the power of your light.

But as we allow our lights to shine and as we sparkle, we must always point the way back to our light source. Jesus is our light source. We don't sparkle for ourselves. We sparkle so that others can see our light source within us.

Remember this:

"A warrior sparkles because of her light source" ~ a Sherryism

God has called us to be warriors and carriers of His light. Amen.

Every warrior has a calling and a purpose. Our callings and our purposes are all different. I cannot preach like other warriors can. I cannot give exhortations like other warriors can. I do not have the anointing to lead praise and worship. My calling is to be an encourager, and I can do that all day.

I am writing this to encourage you that today is better than yesterday and that tomorrow will be better than today. Keep on keeping on. Get off your seat of doing nothing, stand up, and do something. I am writing this to encourage you to become the victorious warrior you were called to be.

Stop allowing your circumstances or other people in your life to hold you back from your calling. Stop listening to the lies of the enemy that are saying you are not enough, because *you are enough*. Stop allowing yourself to doubt that God even knows who you are and what you are going through.

In bringing this chapter to a close, I want to share Psalm 193:1–18 with you. It reads,

> Oh Lord, you have examined my heart and know everything about me. You know when I sit down or stand up. You know my thoughts even when I'm far away. You see me when I travel and when I rest at home. You know everything I do. You know what I am going to say, even before I say it, Lord. You go before me and follow me. You place your hand of blessing on my head. Such knowledge is too wonderful for me, too great for me to understand. I can never escape from your Spirit. I can never get away from your presence. If I ride the wings of the morning, if I dwell by the farthest oceans, even there, your hand will guide me, and your

strength will support me. I could ask the darkness to hide me and the light around me to become night – but even in darkness I cannot hide from you. To you, the night shines as bright as the day. Darkness and light are the same to you. You made all the delicate, inner parts of my body, and knit me together in my mother's womb. Thank you for making me so wonderfully complex. Your workmanship is marvelous – how well I know it. You watched me as I was being formed in utter seclusion, as I was woven together in the dark of the womb. You saw me before I was born. Every day of my life was recorded in your book. Every moment was laid out before a single day had passed. How precious are your thoughts about me, Oh God. They cannot be numbered. I can't even count them. They outnumber the grains of sand. When I wake up, you are still with me. (NLT)

My response to this passage of scripture is ... wow.

I hope that after reading this you will become

aware of just how special you are to God and how very much He wants to see you live as the victorious warrior you were made to be.

As I said before, but would like to remind you again. When we are living every day in fellowship with the Lord, we position ourselves in a place of continuous victory. This means that when the enemy brings battle to you, you do not go out *looking* for the victory. Rather, you *bring the victory to the battle.* How? It's simple. When you are in fellowship with the Great I Am, you are in a constant mode of victory. You are never without it.

Your enemy knows this. He tries to convince you that you *do not have* victory, that you have *never had* victory, and that you *will never have* victory. Yet all the time he is telling you this, he knows you do. He knows that it is already a done deal.

If we could only grasp and keep our minds set on this level of victory acknowledgement, what could we accomplish? Praise the Lord, today and forevermore. The victory is not ahead of us, but rather, it is here now.

Isaiah 12:2 reads, "The Lord God is my strength and my song He has given me Victory" (NLT).

Me and Jimmie

My girls as
Wonder Woman
Warriors!
Bethany, Ammanda
and Charity
(Carly)

Grandson Josh,
Jimmie,
Me and
Grandson Hunter

Me and Rev. Frances Williams

My sister, Laurita and I
Having a fun
Lunch

My daughter, Bethany,
me and my sister,
Laurita cooking mama's
recipe for fried oysters!

My daughter,
Charity (Carly)
and me
celebrating our
birthdays

Me, Daughter
Bethany, Jimmie,
Grandson
Josh, Grandson
Hunter
celebrating
Josh's birthday

Me and Beautiful Bestie, Donna Bach enjoying lunch together

Me with my new favorite rolling pin – "Just Roll With It!" Gotta make things taste better, right?!

Beautiful
Warrior Girlfriend,
Deborah (Debbie)
Donnelly

Deborah
(Debbie)
Donnelly and
her Dad, Walt
Reynolds.

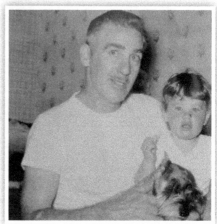

Our Christmas
cards for 2020
Spoiler alert!

Celebrating my
68th birthday,
flowers from
my daughter
Bethany

Beautiful
Warrior
Girlfriend,
Carol Doppler
and I having
lunch together

Beautiful
Warrior
Girlfriend,
Cat Gillham
and I
Enjoying
a dress up
tea party in
my home

My Bestie, Tari Nixon and I having fun in a
pottery class and sight-seeing in Sedona, AZ.

My
Beautiful
BFF

Jennifer Raskovich

Me and Bestie, Sue Horn, having a fun evening of games and what else...Taco Potato Chips!

Beautiful
Warrior Girlfriend,
Marilyn Reynolds

Beautiful
Warrior Girlfriend,
Carolyn Jones
Thompson

Beautiful
Warrior Girlfriend,
Linda Grossman

Me and my Hubby
and Best Friend

Chapter 6

Beautiful Warrior Girlfriends

Warriors are those who choose to stand between their enemy and all that she loves or holds sacred.

If you have read my previous seven books, you know I love talking about my girlfriends. The "Beautiful Warrior Girlfriends " chapter in this book is somewhat bittersweet for me because two of my very closest friends have recently gone to be with Jesus. They have left a huge hole in my life, but they have forever written their names on my heart. Nickie Brown Blanford and Rita Jean Tipton-Henrich, it is a privilege to honor you in "Beautiful Warrior Girlfriends." Love to you always.

I was visiting my precious and best friend, Nickie, during the last days of her battle with cancer. She told me, "I feel like I'm on a slippery slide."

I answered, "Well, eventually we hit the ground on our bottoms, right?" By that, I meant we all, at one time or another, feel out of control on the slippery slide. We know that eventually, the slide stops, the descent ends, and we land. Nickie lost her battle with cancer, and in her honor, I want to share my thoughts of her.

Nickie Brown Blanford

Nickie is my truest of besties. What can I say about Nickie that those who know her don't already know? We were sisters-in-love. We met through our kids. Her son fell in love with my daughter and vice versa. One of my first memories of Nickie was when our kids asked both sets of parents to have lunch with them at The Farm in Ahwatukee, Arizona. It was the first time we were introduced to each other, and I knew right away that Nickie was someone special and that I wanted to get to know her better.

We had a lot in common. We shared a love

for the color purple, adored our families, and unashamedly loved Jesus. The kids dragged their feet but eventually had their dream wedding. Almost immediately afterward, Nickie and I became great friends.

I cherish the beautiful pieces of jewelry that she made for me. She once asked me if I had any amethysts. I told her that I did not. She immediately pulled out a fabulous pair of amethyst earrings she had made. As she gave them to me, she told me, "Every woman needs amethysts." That was Nickie. That woman loved her jewelry.

We met monthly for lunch and therapy shopping. We loved to eat. We talked, laughed, hugged, and prayed together over our children and grandchildren. We had dress-up tea parties. We had lunch at quaint tearooms. We went junking. She got hooked on teacups.

We were sisters from the heart. She was a no-nonsense God-is-who-He-says-He-is kind of a girl. Even though Nickie was allergic to most flowers, she was the sweetest flower of them all. Her sweet fragrance lingers, and it will always be with us.

Nickie left behind a legacy for her children and grandchildren: She wanted them to find out who they are in Jesus and then to be that. That's what she wanted. Nickie is in our past, but she is also this very moment, in our future. If I know Nickie, she is probably giving Jesus a few ideas of what each one of us needs in our mansion.

Five days before Nickie went to heaven, I brought her a silver fork. That fork was part of my mama's wedding service. You see, I told Nickie a story I had heard of a young woman, who was walking her journey home to be with Jesus. She asked her pastor to come to her house to help her make all the final arrangements.

Before he left her house, she gave him a fork. She told him that she wanted to be holding the fork during her memorial service. He asked why. She told him that when she was a little girl, her grandmother would tell her that when the main course was being cleared away, she should hang on to her fork because something wonderful was about to be served. The best was yet to come. Dessert was on its way.

Nickie held on to that fork as she said her goodbyes. It helped her keep her eyes on the goal: dessert with Jesus. The best was yet to come. Nickie told her family that she was going to have crème brulee and raspberries with Jesus. Nickie, I love you so much. Enjoy your dessert. This story stays with me. It haunts me. Every time I place forks on the table for my loved ones to use, I think of this story.

***

This past year, I have said my earthly goodbyes to two of my very close besties. I have eaten with them, laughed with them, and cried with them. I cherish the forks that they used. I cherish the fact that they have entered into the everlasting beauty of heaven, and they are now worshipping the King of kings and Lord of lords. They are using their forks and experiencing the best that is theirs for eternity.

I hope that you will remember this story and realize that whatever you believe is the best thing you have ever experienced cannot compare with what the Lord has prepared for you ... so keep your fork.

Rita Jean Tipton-Henrich

To truly sparkle, your soul must sparkle. Therefore, you must give your soul permission to sparkle. If anyone has ever sparkled, it was my longtime friend Rita Jean.

Rita and I met when we were young adults. Her father was a preacher, and she and her siblings were an anointed, talented singing group. We had a lot in common, since my dad was also a preacher, and I, like Rita, sang with my siblings.

Rita and I didn't stay in touch while raising our families and navigating through life. But one day,

I received an online message from this blast from the past. It was Rita Jean. I began to call her Rita Jean immediately, which was my special name for her. Almost no one called her by both her first and middle name, but to me, Rita was this amazing, strong force, who needed to be called by two names. Her love for Jesus and unashamed worship of Him blessed me.

It was common for us to meet up for lunch and junking. That girl would, out of nowhere, begin to bellow out a song of praise and adoration for her Lord and Savior. Bless her heart. She loved Jesus, and she didn't care who knew it. She had talent. Not many people in this world have the heavy anointing and strong vocal ability that Rita Jean owned. I know she has been singing her heart out since she moved to heaven.

Rita became ill with pancreatic cancer and survived only a couple months. She wouldn't talk about it to me. We would talk about life and not death.

Just about a week before she moved to heaven, I went to visit my beautiful friend. We had a dress-up tea party. Rita Jean loved coming to my home, dressing up, and having high tea. So I took a couple of my vintage furs, hats, and gloves, and we had our tea party, which included burgers that day. After our tea party, we strolled around, had a

Southern Belle parade, took communion together, and polished our toes.

From start to finish, that day was very special and full of sparkles, love, and laughter. It was our last day together on this earth. I cherish every moment that we had. I am thankful that we had time to say, "I love you and see ya soon." I refused to say goodbye.

Rita was a talker. That girl loved to talk. Her laugh was spontaneous and infectious. But it was her unbelievable heart that drew me to her. I thought that when God brought her back into my life, we would have many, many years of memories. But He got her mansion ready faster than anyone could imagine. Fly high and sing loud, beautiful Rita Jean. I miss you every day.

***

Does it ever occur to you that we women seem to live in seasons? First, we are our mother's daughter. We struggle with finding our own identities. For some, there is a season of complete and unimaginable love and utter chaos while raising our children. We blink, and before our eyes, we become empty nesters floundering around and again trying to find our own identities.

Then if we are fortunate, we are blessed to become grandmothers.

There are seasons of extreme loss and overwhelming despair. There are seasons of joy and jubilation beyond our wildest dreams. Our hands, which were small and smooth, become worn and wrinkled with the journey of life. I have friends in all stages of life, and I have experienced all stages. But girls, I am in no way an expert. I made some ridiculous and complete messes along the way.

But I do know that I am here to encourage every friend, no matter what season you are finding yourself in. Why? Because there is strength in numbers. You alone might be struggling, but when I show up, I can hold your arms up in victory when they become tired. That's what I do. I will be your encourager, supporter, sounding board, and shoulder to cry on. I will cry with you during the battle, and I will dance and rejoice with you when victory comes.

By being you, you encourage me. For example, let me introduce you to my mentor and adopted mother in the Lord, Rev. Frances Williams.

Rev. Frances Williams

It is my great honor to introduce to you this powerful woman of God: Rev. Frances Williams, who is the wife of Bill Williams and the mother of Magdalene, Winston, and Calvin. In 1960, Frances Williams surrendered her life to the Lord and received the baptism of the Holy Spirit. She was ordained for ministry in Englewood, New Jersey, in 1962. In her early years of ministry, she organized an interdenominational and interracial prayer band. This step of obedience paved the way for many salvations, miracles, and healings.

In 1973, Sister Williams and her family moved to Arizona and began a ministry of cultural and ethnic diversity. At that time, she came into my life. She has counseled my family, stood in the gap, and prayed for us many, many times. She was my mom's best friend. She stayed with my mom until my mom took her last breath. She picked up the slack when my sister and I could not go on.

In 1988, her husband and life partner, Bill, went to be with the Lord. In this new season of her life, God made a way for her to go back to school. She obtained an associate degree with honors from Chandler-Gilbert Community College and a bachelor's degree in psychology from Northern

Arizona University. She received the honor of valedictorian of her graduating class.

After graduation, Sister Williams's new vision True Hope Anointed Ministries was born, which continues today. She continues to travel nationally and internationally, ministering to diverse denominations and cultures. She has ministered to the American Indian communities for over thirty years, and presently, she is pastoring the Pima Indian Nation and seven other tribes on the Gila River Indian Reservation in Arizona.

I soooo love this woman. She may be little, but she is a mighty warrior in the eyes of God.

Carolyn Adair

> *Nor do they light a lamp and put it under a basket, but on a lampstand, and it gives light to all who are in the house.* (Matthew 5:14 NKJV)

One of the brightest lights I have ever met is my friend Carolyn Adair. You met Carolyn in my book *Your Crown Slips So What Sparkle On*. Carolyn is one of those rare people who, once you meet her, you immediately become close friends with her. She is such a support to me. My journey has been easier and more complete since Carolyn started walking it with me.

I know that when I call, she will stop what she is doing and listen to me. After she listens, she will take me to the throne of God and will petition the Lord for my needs. She has become a sister in every sense of the word. I treasure my friendship with her.

Carolyn is a very sensitive and compassionate woman. I believe this is partially due to her being teased and made fun of when she was in school because she was a Cherokee. Times were different then. Today, she and I both embrace our Cherokee-American heritage.

Carolyn has a ministry that helps women. She taught a women's Bible study group for several years. She loves to make special events available to the men and women who attend her church.

Her husband, Don, and her daughter, Sherry, were healed of cancer. Carolyn has experienced the healing power of God many times. She has many testimonies, and she is bold when witnessing about God-given miracles.

Carolyn has lived in Oklahoma most of her life, and she knows firsthand about living through a tornado. She has survived two of them. One took the life of her grandmother. The other blew her neighbor's barn into Carolyn's bedroom. Every year that she lives through the storm season in Tornado Alley, she sees God's mercy and protection renewed in her life, which gives her more reasons to praise Him.

When Carolyn was younger, she was asked out on a date by a famous young man (If I told you, you would know him immediately). Let's just say, he is a well-known country-music singer. She made such an impression on him, he named a song for her (No, I cannot tell you the name of the song, or you will know exactly who it was). I am so thankful that I can call Carolyn my friend and sister. I cherish her part of my journey.

Check out the "Fiesta Lime Chicken and Rice Bowl", "Cherry Chocolate Cake," and "Cider Glazed Carrots with Walnuts" recipes in the last chapter of the book. They are some of her favorites.

Donna Bach

You met Donna in my first book *Faith, Family, Friends and Fried Chicken*. Donna is a rare human. She has always been a friend who was there for me, no matter what.

She encourages me, lifts me up, laughs with me, cries with me, and always tells me the truth, even though I sometimes don't want to hear it. I think it is why I gravitate to her on a constant basis. There are no games played. She loves me for who I am and accepts that I'm not a perfect human. I'm flawed and quirky, and that's okay with her. We have known each other for decades.

A few months ago, I was in the middle of a physical battle. I was working through some confusion and cloudiness regarding what was going on. This girl wisely said, "Remember, doctors practice their professions." Wow, this was the lightning bolt that I needed to hear. It made me realize that I must trust God as He practices His profession more than I trust humans as they practice theirs. This might not have been what she thought I would take away from her lightning bolt, but I felt that she spoke clarity into a situation of doubt. That's Donna. She is a no-nonsense kind of girl, and I love her dearly.

Donna loves to quilt, and she sews some amazing creations. She has blessed me with several of them. Last year, she brought me one that has meant the world to me. I had seen blankets with scripture on them, and I had a deep desire to have one. But I could never find anything that even came close to what I had seen.

Then one Saturday out of the blue, Donna and her husband, Mark, popped in. She had made me an incredible quilt with scripture verses and positive quotes all over it. She had personalized it with my initials. I was surprised, humbled, and honored that she loved me that much.

I hadn't told anyone that I had been yearning to be under the scriptures, but my bestie was being God's hands extended and was giving me the most beautiful scripture quilt that I had ever seen. That girl was definitely in tune with Jesus when she had made her amazing creation for me. I cherish and use it all the time.

I'm so blessed to call her my friend and my bestie. Check out her recipe in Chapter 8 called "Artichoke Cream Cheese Dip."

Deborah Donnelly

Have you ever met someone, and you were instantly drawn to that person's bright light and amazing heart? This is what happened when God placed Deb in my life.

She lives in Florida. I reside in Arizona. We met through Facebook, and we have become fast and furious friends. I feel as though I've known her all my life. We have a sister connection.

Deb volunteers at a homeless shelter and a pregnancy center. You will understand the importance of this as you continue to read about my friend.

Her story is an over-the-top example of our

Heavenly Father's love and of the manifestation of two scriptures.

> I knew you before I formed you in your mother's womb. Before you were born I set you apart. (Jeremiah 1:5 NLT)

> For I know the plans I have for you says the Lord. They are plans for good and not for disaster to give you a future and a hope. (Jeremiah 29:11 NLT)

My beautiful friend has graciously allowed me to tell a small part of her incredible love story. After eight years of marriage, Deborah was diagnosed with cervical cancer. She then endured a radical hysterectomy. The surgery saved her precious life but dashed her dream of having a baby.

But she didn't give up on her dream of being a mommy. Instead, she handed it over to God. She and her husband, Jim, placed their name in all the adoption agencies in her area. She knew some couples had been on the lists for more than seven years. The reason was that more young mothers were choosing abortion over adoption. With God, there is most assuredly always a but. But miracle of miracles happened.

Deborah and Jim waited less than a year. Jim had been praying for a little girl with red hair. On Valentine's Day (how appropriate that it was the love day), these two precious children of God received a phone call. They were informed that they were now the proud parents of a beautiful baby girl. Their gift of immeasurable love from their Heavenly Father had been born on another special day, December 25, Christmas day. Praise the Lord for His faithfulness.

Their beautiful daughter, Erica, who in my opinion is the spitting image of my beautiful friend Deborah, is the joy of Deborah and Jim's life. Even though they became a family over twenty-nine years ago, not a day has gone by when these parents don't embrace the miraculous intervention and immeasurable gift of love that was bestowed on them: their baby.

Deborah, Jim, and Erica's story brings me tears of joy every time I think of them. With those tears comes a renewed confidence in the magnitude of God's love for His kids. In sharing just this small part of their incredible journey, I hope your faith is restored and increased so that you will believe and receive the fulfillment of the dream you have been promised.

Remember, our Heavenly Father sings joyful songs over us (see Zephaniah 3:17 NLT). I can't wait to meet my fabulous and funny friend in person. I will hug her and not let go. I'm so blessed and honored to call her my friend. God knew I needed her in my life.

Look for these much-loved recipes from her dad, Walt, in the last chapter: "Walt's Famous New York Potato Salad," "Rutabagas," "Red Cabbage and Apples," and "Sex in a Pan Cake." They are some of Deborah's family's favorites (Don't forget to check out the picture of Debbie's dad in the photo gallery as well).

Carol Doppler

Carol and I met a few years ago through an online social website. We live in the same small community. We have lunch together and enjoy each other's company. Carol makes beautiful jewelry and loves to knit. She is very active in a weekly Bible study group.

I asked Carol if I could share some of her miraculous journey with you. Carol received a liver transplant a year or so ago. This in itself was a miracle. She was on the national liver transplant list only three days before she received her new liver. During and after the transplant, Carol developed severe complications. She was hospitalized for seven months. She has many testimonies of what she endured, but this one really touches my heart.

Carol shares,

Being in the hospital for a very long time had moments of ugliness. I was crying daily at some points, and the psychologist asked what I would do if I were home. I told her I would crochet. But some of the surgeries left one hand shaking and the other with neuropathy.

It took a while to finally just insist that this disease was *not* going to win. I asked people to bring me yarn every time they asked if I needed anything, and they did. It was very difficult and frustrating at first, so much so, the therapists questioned it.

As I persisted, my hands began to remember what to do. I was finally able to get one small project done, and the staff was so excited, but I wasn't. My thinking was that it should not have taken me so long. I was determined to get my ability back, so I kept going. I would stay up all night at times, just to reach a small goal that I had set for myself, such as, *I'm doing at least five rows today no matter what.* I would lie to the nurses, telling them I could not sleep, when in reality, it was an internal battle.

After a few weeks, I was really getting my groove back. I was making slippers, hats, blankets, and whatever came to my mind. Eventually, staff members of all sorts were popping in to see what I was working on. Some began requesting items. They would try to pay me, but I refused money. I would take payment in the form of a Coke (dark sodas were not available on my floor). As another form of payment, I would ask for specific meds to be put off for an hour to go roam around the gift shop or walk with my husband. I'd ask for Italian ice, which was my ultimate weakness.

At one point, I had so much yarn and items in my room that one nurse aid said it looked like a yard sale. Yarn is

my happy place. It was my challenge,
but it was very much worth it.

Today my friend is the picture of health. She knows that she has been given a second chance to live, and live she does. I am blessed beyond measure to call Carol my friend. Check out her recipes in Chapter 8: "Chicken Enchiladas with Green Sauce," "Posole," and "Zucchini Bread."

Cat Gillham

Stay close to people who feel like sunlight. (author unknown)

I am continually amazed at how God causes divine interventions to bring girlfriends together. This was the case for me and Cat. She was like a beautiful ray of sunlight when she entered my life.

A few years ago, my husband surprised me with a stay at a bed and breakfast for my birthday. I had never stayed in one before, and it had always been on my wish list of things to experience. The bed and breakfast was in a perfect historical Victorian home, which was situated among the pines of Prescott, Arizona. Prescott is a little over an hour from our home.

When we drove out of the heat of the desert

and into the coolness of the pines and greenness of the quaint town, it was like a breath of fresh air. We soaked up the ambiance of the bed and breakfast and the town while sitting on the large front porch. Everything about the visit was magical.

The next morning, I met Cat. Oh my goodness, talk about a God thing and a divine appointment. At the time, I didn't know just how important she would become to me and the friendship we would have together. We bonded immediately.

Cat was the chef at the bed and breakfast. After she served us her awesome breakfast quiche, she began to visit with us. Unbeknownst to me, she had looked me up on my website. She began asking me about my books. She was a member of one of the book clubs in Prescott, and she purchased several books from me that morning.

God used Cat to open a door for me to eventually speak at her book club, and what a great time it was. When I arrived at the book club's meeting, to my surprise and delight, I saw that each woman had chosen a recipe from one of my several books. I was treated to a fabulous luncheon of love and culinary talents from this group of women. After feasting on the buffet of deliciousness, we had a fabulous one-on-one discussion. I will be forever grateful to Cat for bringing about these new friendships.

A year or so later, I hosted high tea for some of the ladies from this group. They dressed up and came to my home. What a privilege it was to give back to these beautiful ladies.

Cat and I continue to meet up for lunch and antique shopping. She is such an anointed woman of God. She is full of faith, so no matter what the circumstance, God is still and will forever be in control. She makes me feel safe and secure in that knowledge. I know that she prays for me constantly. This makes me a better person.

I love this girl so much. She has snuggled into my heart, and she will always be loved and adored. I always look forward to our visits. If I could give you an example of a Proverbs 31 woman, it would be Cat. Her Proverbs 31 spirit encourages me and is a balm to everyone she encounters.

Try these delicious recipes from Cat: "Cat's Mexican Corn Bread Waffles," "Hatch Green Chili Chicken Breakfast Casserole," "Spinach and Kale Quiche with Sweet Potato Crust," and "Thanksgiving and Christmas Soup." They are in the last chapter of this book. You will be glad you did.

Linda Grossman

Linda is another friend that I have been blessed to meet through social media. I stand amazed at how God brings us together. Distance is not a factor to Him and His family. He knows exactly whom He wants His kids to meet. It doesn't matter if you are a shut-in or live in a remote place. He brings His kids together at a time in their journey when they need each other. Linda was brought into my life at such a time.

We are sisters in every sense of the word. We are family. We love and support each other. We pray together. We laugh together, and we encourage each other.

Linda was born and raised on a farm. She tells me that she is definitely not a girly girl (like I am). She milked cows, bailed hay, mowed grass, and did anything else that was needed to help her parents. She learned to ride horseback when she was in diapers (Bless her heart).

She loves to be outside in the woods and under the trees. She also loves animals. She is also an avid reader. Among her many talents are sewing, crafting, baking, and cooking. She is also a giver. She cooks for the staff at her church, and she has done it every month for years. Linda tells me she knows that God has always protected her, worked out her problems, and provided for her. Be sure and check out Linda's recipes in Chapter 8: "Chocolate Marshmallow Pie," "Pecan Pie," and "Pumpkin Pie."

Susan Horn

I met Sue right after Jimmie and I married. Her husband, Mike, worked with Jimmie, and they had been friends for several years before we were married.

Sue is an amazing woman. She is beautiful, kind, soft spoken, and full of life and laughter. Sue teaches second grade. I'm amazed at what she does and I tell her that it has to be a calling during these days. I can't imagine the stress yet the joy she receives every day.

Her husband recently broke his back and endured a four-month stay in the hospital. During this time, Mike stated that Sue was his rock. He says that he wouldn't be where he was today without her.

The way he loves, adores, and praises her reminds me of the Proverbs 31 woman scripture.

> She is clothed with strength and dignity, and she laughs without fear of the future. When she speaks

her words are wise and she gives instructions with kindness. She carefully watches everything in her household and suffers nothing from laziness. Her children stand and bless her. Her husband praises her (saying) there are many virtuous and capable women in the world, but you surpass them all. (Proverbs 31:25–29 NLT)

When I read this scripture, I think of another girlfriend, I think of Sue. She teaches little ones with wise words and gives instruction with kindness. Her husband definitely knows the jewel that she is. So do I. I love this girl, and I'm glad she is in my life.

We make time to visit on a regular basis, whether it is participating in a couples dinner and game night or a girl's day of junking and lunch. It is good to have close friends that you can travel with during life's journey. I couldn't ask for a better one.

Please check out Sue's recipes in Chapter 8: "Dill Pickle Dip," "Bacon Cheese Fries," "Fifties-Style Salisbury Steak," and "Pistachio Cake."

Tari Nixon

"I didn't find my friends; the good Lord gave them to me." - Ralph Waldo Emerson

I love this quote by Ralph Waldo Emerson. I find the way that the Lord brings us into each other's lives truly amazing. This is so true when it comes to my lifelong and best friend, Tari Nixon.

God gave me the gift of Tari in the early 1980s. It was one of the darkest times of my life. It was a chapter of struggle, emotional and physical abuse, and learning to survive when life was difficult.

She was a social worker at a local community mental health center in Anadarko, Oklahoma. I was hired as the executive secretary/administrative assistant. We formed a tight bond immediately and became best friends for life.

She was the sustaining force that gave me courage to make difficult decisions and to finally find peace. Together, we have gone through highs and lows and valleys and mountaintops. Our journey together is one of mutual respect and enormous love for each other.

She lives in Salem, Oregon now, and I reside in Arizona. But we make it a priority to visit each other at least once a year. When we do have the pleasure of being together, we cram every minute with fun, laughter, and adventures.

A few years ago we took a road trip to the quaint town of Sedona, Arizona. The majesty of the area was beyond words. Of course, we had to hit all the thrift stores along the way. No trip is complete without junking. We also tried our hand at potter's wheels. We took a class in clay art and developed what we thought was great skill in pottery making.

One evening, I was getting ready to retire for the night when I heard a knock on my bedroom door. I opened the door, and Tari was standing there trying to be somewhat serious. She asked me, "Did the rug in my room come with the sparkles?"

Oh my goodness, I have laughed repeatedly over this remark every time I think about that night. My sheepish reply was, "Uh, no, it did not come with sparkles."

We both chuckled as she turned to walk back into her room and remarked, "I was just wondering. I didn't think so." While the rug did not come with sparkles, we all know how much I love glitter and sparkles. When you use sparkles a lot, they are just bound to fall where they may.

Something else happened during her last visit that I thought was another gift from God. After all, He controls the wind and the rain. On her last day, it began to rain. It was not the rainy season in Arizona. Rain was not in the forecast, but rain it did. It came down in sheets. It began to thunder—wonderful deep-throated thunder.

I thought this was spectacular because Tari loves thunderstorms as much as I do, and she doesn't get to experience them in Salem. It thundered and rained all the way to the airport. What a great ending to a fabulous visit. It was kind of like God gave His stamp of approval and a little extra blessing to my friend as she visited the dry desert of Arizona.

Tari keeps very busy in Salem. She is part of a book club, takes frequent get-a-way trips to the Oregon coast's beaches. She knits, sews, makes quilts, loves her Goodwill junking adventures, and attends many plays, concerts, and art and social events. She is always just a phone call away, whenever we need to talk to and be there for each other.

Tari shares her love of quilting with me. She tells me that sometimes, she takes a piece of material and purposely sews it upside down on the quilt to make the quilt both unique and different—not perfect. She sews on buttons, ribbons, lace, and anything that brings it to its quirky self. She says, "No quilt is perfect, only God makes perfect things." I am blessed beyond measure to share life with such an intriguing and loving girlfriend.

Please check out these recipes in the last chapter of this book: "Joyce's Lemon Pie," "Potato Cheese Puffs," "Cinnamon Roll Bread Pudding," "Chicken Noodle Chops," and "Dirty Strawberries." These are some of her family's favorites.

Jennifer Raskovich

You met my BFF Jennifer in my very first book, *Faith, Family, Friends & Fried Chicken.* She has been a constant in my life for several years now.

During the time right after I had lost Nickie and Rita Jean from my life, I pulled away from everyone. That pulling away included Jen, and it hurt her deeply. She couldn't understand, and I couldn't explain. But Jen is the very essence of the forgiving power of Jesus.

After I worked through my uncertainty, pain, and grief, I realized that I had hurt the ones I loved the most. Jen forgave me, and now our friendship is even stronger than before. I love her. I love spending time with her. We share the same love for junking, eating, shopping, talking, and the power of friendship.

Jen and my adventures begin the minute she gets in my car. She holds on for dear life.

There have been times she would get the courage to whisper, "that was a red light you just went through" or the latest "you are on the wrong side of the road". Bless her heart. She is my main gal!

The power of friendship is a very unique power. Jen and I share this uncanny ability that we pretty much understand what the other is going to say before they say it. Everyone needs a friend who loves her and supports her like Jen does me.

I am so proud of Jen. This past year, she has worked hard and has lost one hundred pounds. She looks amazing. Her health has improved, and her attitude and outlook on life is much more positive. Kudos to you, Jen. You are amazing. I love you, girlfriend. Please check out her recipes in Chapter 8: "Pimento Cheese Spread," "Peanut Butter Fudge," and "Chocolate Fantasy Fudge."

Marilyn Reynolds

This past year, I received an email through my website from a beautiful child of God. She had purchased several of my books. We began to communicate back and forth. Then of all surprises, she told me her maiden name, and it surprised me. She had been a very sweet and beautiful friend who had attended the same church my family had worshipped at when we were teenagers.

I couldn't believe it. How, after all these years, did she find me? I believe it was a divine intervention. God loves to surprise us this way.

This woman had been a beautiful young lady when we had last seen each other. Now, she was a gorgeous, mature Christian, who had raised her family, and like me, was going through the same life issues.

After the final shock of reconnecting in such a miraculous way, we began our friendship right where we had left it. She made me laugh one day when she reminded me,

> Sherry, we thought your family was so much more religious than ours. I remember you could not use nail polish or even nail polish remover (which we used to take scuff marks off our white shoes). And I remember when you guys came over to play games, you couldn't play with dice. So we had to use spinners when you came.

Bless her heart. She made me laugh. My parents did not raise us with the grace of God but rather with the mindset of works and a whole lot of no's. (Bless their hearts).

When Marilyn shared these memories with me, I realized that I had forgotten all about them. She opened a whole new memory lane for me. I find it amazing that we only remember small moments in our lives that stay with us for a lifetime. I have a quote on a bedroom wall in my house that reads, "We don't remember days, we remember moments" (unknown).

Marilyn is such a blessing to me. Her walk with the Lord encourages me to dig deeper. I am so thankful God brought her back into my life. Check out Marilyn's family's favorite recipes: "Buttermilk Pancakes" and "Buttermilk Biscuits."

Carolyn Thompson

Carolyn is another friend who I have been privileged to meet through social media. It is amazing how it can bring women into my life who are kindred souls and who immediately become close friends.

Carolyn told me that she worked at a rehabilitation facility as a cook. During that time, she discovered that she could make backpacks. She began small. She made them for her grandkids to take to school. Carolyn's facilities manager saw the bags and suggested that Carolyn begin to make them as wheelchair bags and to sell them.

She bought a pattern and tried making them. It came easy to Carolyn. She told me that it only took one and a half yards of fabric for each bag. The first time, she made fifteen of them. Carolyn said,

> It was November, and I was going to my brother's in Tulsa for Thanksgiving. It happened that my niece had recently gone to work at a veterans' center in Claremore. I decided to take them to her. That night, she told me they cried and said that no one ever thought of them. Then I cried. It's the least I could do.

Carolyn tells me that she read this phrase somewhere: "Only two defining forces ever died for you. Jesus Christ, and the American Soldier. One for your soul, the other for your freedom." It struck a chord within Carolyn.

As of this date, Carolyn has made one hundred of them, and all but eight have gone to veterans. The eight went to family and friends. She prays over and puts this poem in the pocket of each one.

I said a prayer for you today and know God must have heard I felt the answer in my heart although He spoke no word. I didn't ask for wealth or fame, I knew you wouldn't mind, I asked Him to send treasures of a far more lasting kind. I asked that He be near you at the start of each new day. To grant you, health and blessings and friends to share your way. I asked for happiness for you in all things great and small. But it was for His loving care I prayed the most of all." —author unknown

Sewing the wheelchair bags for veterans is now Carolyn's vision and mission. She sent me nineteen recently. My husband and I were privileged to be Carolyn's hands. It was an honor to personally deliver them to beautiful, deserving heroes in wheelchairs at the Phoenix VA hospital. You cannot imagine the way those veterans' faces lit up and the smiles we received when we gave them Carolyn's gift.

Carolyn is such an inspiration to me. She is the perfect example of being blessed to be a blessing to others. She is a testament that God has many ways for each of us to be that blessing. We are each given special talents. What we do with them, well, that's up to each of us individually. Carolyn has embraced her talents and has become God's hands extended.

Please check out her recipes in Chapter 8. They are "Taco Pizza," "Apple Pie Enchiladas," and "Pumpkin Ice-Cream Pie."

Chapter 7

Joy and Jubilation

"Do life with joy, it confuses the enemy." ~ a Sherryism

And Sarah said, "God hath made me to laugh, so that all that hear will laugh with me." (Genesis 21:6 KJV)

We are told find joy in the journey. Make the choice to rejoice. Scripture tells us, "Always be full of joy in the Lord. I say it again—rejoice" (Philippians 4:4 NLT), and, "The joy of the Lord is our strength" (Nehemiah 8:10 NLT). So this is my thinking: We must look for and find the Lord in order to acquire His joy for our journey. Seeking joy from any other source is superficial, and it does not anchor us in hard times when we need strength.

I remember my Dad telling the story of when he was courting mama. They would be walking down the street in Bardstown or Louisville, Kentucky. Dad would, without notice, begin to skip unashamedly down the sidewalk, hunching his back and shoulders and laughing as he went along. This would invariably embarrass my prim and proper little mama. But dad would keep doing it. He could not contain his joy. He was in love with mama and was so happy that he couldn't contain himself. When walking down the street with her, holding her hand didn't do it for him. He had to skip to release his joy.

This carried on even into his later years. As he preached and ministered the Word of God, he would, without warning, run down the aisle and dance before the Lord. He could not contain his *joy*.

The joy of the Lord cannot be contained. If we are truly in love with Jesus, we will experience a joy such as my dad did. It will bring us to the place where we must release our praise.

Give yourself an attitude check. Straighten your crown and begin to get your praise on. Today you are highly favored and blessed by God. You are sons and daughters of the King. You are a royal prince or princess. He is worthy of and desires to hear your praise.

Praise is one of my favorite things to do. When I am alone at home or in my car, I always have praise and worship music blaring. The louder it is the better it is.

Recently, I was at home, and I decided to click on my praise-and-worship phone playlist. I always play it through my Bluetooth speaker, which changes colors to the music. Well, I was doing my thing in the house, which was praising God as I performed my chores.

All at once, I heard a strange bang. Then it sounded like something rolled a couple of times. With the music still blaring, I walked through each room and looked to see if anything was askew. When I came into the dining room, I saw that my Bluetooth speaker had fallen off the top of the antique radio and had rolled a couple times.

Now, that little escapade didn't affect the speaker whatsoever. Praise and worship was still loudly coming from it. This made me chuckle out loud, and I thought, *Even the speaker had to do a little praise and worship on its own. The top of the radio couldn't hold it back. It was having as good a time as I was.* I can always find a God thing in everything, and I could just picture God chuckling with me.

Never doubt the power of your praise.

Lift up your hands in the sanctuary and praise the Lord. (Psalm 134:2 KJV)

Praise is such an important part in our joy walk with Jesus. Never be ashamed or timid to lift your hands and worship the Lord. It seems to me that the enemy realizes how powerful your praises can be. It is an area that he likes to keep bound up.

I really mean this. When we go to concerts, whether they are country, rock, pop, Christian, or whatever, we get into the music and songs. We lift our hands. We sway with the rhythm. Is that a form of worship? Are any of us ashamed to raise our hands at a concert? Are we timid? Do we look around to see if anyone else is doing it? Are we afraid of what someone will think? Probably not.

Our human instinct is to worship—to respond. When we attend concerts, we don't think twice about raising our hands to the music, so don't ever allow the enemy to make you feel uncomfortable about lifting your hands to worship your Lord and Savior. He is worthy of our praise, and our praise brings victory. There is supernatural power in our praise. Do it. Never be ashamed or timid.

You have a *beyond*. Did you ever think of that?

It is so easy to get wrapped up in the struggles of what we think we can or cannot do. We tend to live in our safe mode. But what if we took off the limits, stopped relying on our own abilities, and relinquished our fears. What would happen then?

God wants to perform a beyond for you. Push through your humanity and open yourself to experience your beyond.

"Where our abilities end, God's abilities begin." ~ a Sherryism

Once, Jimmie and I took a trip to Kentucky to visit some of my relatives. My dad made the trip with us. We rented a car. Because Dad knew every little back road and hog path (as he called them) in the state of Kentucky, he became our chauffeur.

During one of our day trips, we were sitting in a drive-through and waiting for our turn, when Dad looked over at Jimmie, who was riding shotgun, and chuckled, saying, "Well lookie here. Did you see that? The steering wheel just came right off."

Jimmie and I both turned quickly toward Dad and the steering column. Why? Because we were still in the car, and the engine was still running. We were wondering how we were going to get out of the drive-through and on with our journey while Dad was holding the steering wheel in his hands and waving it around. I thought, *What? Oh my goodness. Oh my goodness.*

But having been a professional semi-truck driver for a large part of his life, Dad was not intimidated or bothered by the fact that the steering wheel had come off the steering column. After chuckling, he returned it to its proper place, all while still driving the car. Bless his heart.

What could have been a disaster and a heartbreak was just another bump in the road to Dad, our navigator. Years later as I reminisce about this, I realize that I should be just as comfortable with God being my navigator and steering me through potential disaster and heartbreak.

During that trip, I was not fearful because Dad was driving. Whatever we faced, Dad would handle it. He was a professional. He knew the countryside. He had the knowledge and experience to lead Jimmie and me to our destination that day. I didn't even think twice about helping my Dad navigate. He didn't need my help. He was quite capable of getting us to our destination safely and on time.

Yet in my life journey, I repeatedly try to take the wheel from God and become my own navigator. When I do this, I always get in the way of my true navigator, the Lord. Why is it so hard for me to trust Him with my life in the same way that I trusted my Dad?

There will be times when the steering wheel might come off the column. If I have already given Jesus the control to be my navigator, there is no need to panic. I don't have to lean over, grab the steering wheel, and try to fix it. In fact, I better just leave it alone because if I get involved, I can cause the vehicle to veer out of control and to hit another vehicle or an embankment. None of this is necessary.

Corrie ten Boom once asked, "Is prayer your steering wheel or your spare tire?" My answer to this is, "both." My reasoning for this answer is that in the daily process of traveling our journeys, we should always allow Jesus to do the steering, guiding, and navigating. So yes, prayer should be our steering wheels so that we can be in sync with God and His direction for our journeys.

Yet we should always equip ourselves with prayer, as we would a spare tire. So if life gives us blowouts, Jesus is there as our backup. When we have given Jesus permission to take the wheel and become our navigator, we don't have to worry about becoming lost or not getting home.

This brings to my mind an incident that happened when I first married my husband. I had moved from a very, very, very small town in rural Oklahoma to the hustle and bustle of busy metropolitan Phoenix, Arizona. I was job hunting, and I became dismayed as I tried to conquer the enormous change in driving.

I told my husband, "I don't know how to get there and back to where we are living. I'm so scared I will get lost, and I won't be able to find my way home." It was very frightening to me. At that time, there were no GPS systems in automobiles and no Google to ask directions. We had no cell phones. It was the age of landlines for telephones. The most advanced technology available was a little pager.

So every evening before my next day of interview appointments, my hubby would sit down with me and draw a map. Bless his heart. He would draw a very detailed map of how to get from our home to the place of the interview. Then being the practical that man he was, he would turn the map around and tell me, "Just turn it around and follow it backward to get home." Ha ha! I love this man. What a jewel.

My reason for bringing up this little example is to say that we don't have to be afraid of the drive to the destination when we trust in our navigator. I had to trust that Jimmie would *not* draw me a map that I could not follow or that was bogus and would lead me to nowhere. We must have this same kind of trust in Jesus. He will not draw us a bogus map. Neither will he send us in the wrong direction.

Awhile back, I injured my ankle. I had to keep it bandaged, wear a boot, and walk with crutches for several weeks. During this time, one of my friends, Joyce, injured her leg as well. We were both down at the same time. Both of us are very active hands-on kinds of girls, so we were not happy with the situation. At one point, I told her, "Joyce, I have learned a few tricks with my crutches, and I have also learned a new way to dance my dance."

Don't be discouraged when life throws challenges at you because you are *still you.* Use the experience as a learning-curve lesson and continue to live and do what you have been placed on this earth to do. Don't allow yourself to be despondent or depressed. Instead, allow yourself to become stronger and wiser. Find the joy in it.

I have a friend on Facebook whose profile picture is of her and her hubby riding in a car with the wind blowing her hair back. She looks like she is enjoying the ride of her life, head thrown back, laughing and hair flying in the wind. I just love that picture. I always chuckle when I see it. It reminds me how that is *exactly* the way we should live our lives—top down, wind blowing our hair, and enjoying the ride. Find the joy.

Not too long ago, I was having my alone time with Jesus and I read this verse in the book of Song of Solomon 6:11 (NKJV), which reads "I went down to the garden of nuts." Oh my goodness!

Now I realize the writer meant it exactly as he wrote it. He went to the garden where all the nuts were growing, because the next line reads "to see the verdure of the valley". Verdure means lush, green vegetation.

So yeah, I get it. He wanted to see the beauty of the valley and the valley nearest him was the greenest and most lush. It was the valley where the nuts were growing. It makes total sense.

But that morning, as I read the scripture, it hit me like a lightening bolt. And I began to laugh out loud. How can you read the first line of that scripture and *not* crack up?

In my mind I saw all the fun loving people in my life doing silly things, making me laugh, the nuts in my valley. I saw myself doing my own shenanigans (of which I thoroughly enjoy). Then I realized God absolutely knew that I would read this scripture and receive JOY from His Word.

And it made me wonder, when He anointed the writer to say this, did He know it would make me laugh that day? Of course He did. That's who

God is. He not only loves to the utmost, He has an amazing sense of humor. He knows JOY gives us strength on our journey.

Don't ever think God is just a stern God sitting on His throne with a paddle in His hand. He is the most amazing God. The GREAT I AM.

And yet, He wants to have a relationship with me and you. Even if it takes us to the valley of the nuts. Praise the Lord, today and for ever more.

Too many times, we get in a rut with everyday chores, demands, and responsibilities, and we don't enjoy our journeys. But if we don't practice joy, we miss so much that life has to offer. Put the top down, let your hair blow in the breeze, and begin to enjoy your life. You have this one shot. Make it count. Find the joy.

I once read, "Opportunity dances with those already on the dance floor." That's an interesting concept. What do we do in that scenario? Are we the wallflower who sits alone and wonders why nothing is happening? Are we the ones who get out on life's dance floor and allow ourselves to be the vessel we are meant to be? We don't have to be in the middle of the dance floor, dancing with the most popular guy or gal. We can be alone and on the edge, as long as we get on the floor and dance so we don't miss our opportunity.

When that opportunity arises, do it with

excitement and joy. Don't allow what others think of you to hinder you in your song because your song is not like anyone else's. It's your life, so sing. Find your joy.

King David was so full of joy that he danced half-naked in the street and really embarrassed his wife (She got mad). But he didn't apologize (See 2 Samuel 6 KJV). Now, I'm not saying to toss your clothes, people. But I am saying to practice joy. Meet your situation head-on. Pray. Give it to Jesus. Then sing. Learn to use every negative experience to sing even louder.

James 1:2–3 reads "Consider it pure joy, my brothers and sisters, whenever you face trials of many kinds, because you know that the testing of your faith produces perseverance" (NIV). What is perseverance, and why do we care if our faith produces it? According to the Merriam-Webster dictionary, perseverance is, "Not giving up. It is persistence. The effort required to do something and keep doing it until the end, even if it is hard; despite difficulties, failure and opposition. Steadfastness." In this scripture, James, the younger brother of Jesus is telling us we should consider it pure joy when we face trials.

Well, that is not my mindset when I hit a bump or a pothole on my journey. My first response is usually tears, followed by sadness, and then an oh-poor-me attitude. Sometimes, I get angry. Sometimes, a cloud of despair and depression descends upon me like a thunderstorm in monsoon season. I take my eyes off my goal. I forget to count it pure joy.

But James understood that if we can just get our eyes off ourselves, even when we are in the battle of our lives, and practice joy, our faith grows. It produces *perseverance*. We become steadfast. We endure. We don't give up. Despite difficulties, opposition, and even failure, we are victorious.

We must practice joy over and over and push through to the end, even if it is hard. Nothing is ever accomplished by feeling sorry for ourselves. Our strength is in pure joy.

Isaiah 9:1 reads, "Nevertheless the gloom will not be upon her who is distressed" (NKJV). I absolutely love this. I almost shouted when I read the scripture this week—seriously.

Have you ever been around people who always talk about gloom and doom but never about thankfulness or faith? I have. I don't like it. It feels very uncomfortable to me. They don't even think about joy.

I try not to play into or give much of my time and energy to gloom and doom. I strive to choose faith, joy, and happiness every day. Is my life perfect? Oh my, no, it isn't. Is my family perfect? Goodness gracious, no, it isn't.

We are all humans walking in flesh. But even when we are stressed and distressed, no gloom will be upon us. That's what God's Word says, and I believe and receive this promise. I have the promise from God, and I choose to accept it. Join me. Find your joy.

> Therefore, with joy you will draw water from the wells of salvation. (Isaiah 12:3 NKJV)

Nehemiah 8:10 reads, "The Joy of the Lord is your strength" (NKJV). I can handle the hard stuff much easier when I tackle it in my joy walk and not my carnal walk. My carnal person gets me in trouble. But victory comes from the strength of the Lord, which flows from His joy.

God is not a god of sadness. In fact, when God allowed Jesus to be beaten and to carry His cross after being beaten, Jesus actually fell under the load and heaviness of the cross. He didn't fall because he was weak—absolutely not. He was the Son of God. What made him fall was the fact that He was not only carrying a cross, but He was carrying all the sadness in the world. He was carrying your sadness—your every tear. He was carrying my sadness.

Get this: He was carrying it so we (you and I) would NEVER have to. Catch a glimpse of that truth. He was making a way for our joy walk. So why can't we give Him all the things that hold us down in the mully-grubs? Only then will we begin to walk out our own joy walks.

We don't really like detours, do we? When we are on a trip and see yellow signs and orange cones, we get a little agitated or apprehensive. We think, *Great, this is all I need. Now what? I don't need this. I wonder what is going on.* These thoughts bounce into our brain.

This is similar to what happens on our spiritual journeys. There will be detours, and when they show up, remember to trust God and to not complain. Embrace what you first thought was a nuisance, a waste of time, not part of the game plan, and way off the chosen route because it is still part of God's plan for you. He knows how to navigate you through the obstacles.

"*Sometimes the blessing is in the detour.*" ~ a Sherryism

We could, on the other hand, not embrace the detour. Do we really want His will or do we want to hold on to *our* will, even if it isn't what the Lord wants? This could be one of the reasons why we sometimes say, "God doesn't answer my prayers. I don't see Him working for me. I don't know why I pray. He never listens to me. I don't believe He cares about me."

Warriors, could this be happening because we don't take time to really seek His will and His plan even if it includes a detour? Could it be that we just say prayers of, "Give me this. I need you to do this"? He probably won't turn our water into Starbucks coffee, but that doesn't mean He can't. So trust Him, even in the detour. Find your joy.

Just remember that the enemy doesn't waste his time on someone who is wishy-washy or lukewarm. Wishy-washiness isn't going to do anything for Jesus, and it is not a threat to the devil's cause. Because he knows the Bible better than most of us do, he knows God says that if we are lukewarm, He will "spit us out of His mouth" (Revelation 3:16 NLT), much like we do a lukewarm soda. We usually want our beverages really cold or hot but never lukewarm. Lukewarm doesn't usually give us any pleasure. When we fall into a lukewarm relationship with the Lord, it doesn't give Him any pleasure. So that's fine with the enemy.

But when we are diligently reading our Bibles,

studying, praying fervently, and believing, professing, and standing on God's promises, watch out. We are preparing for a spiritual war. We are preparing for a confrontation with the enemy. Know this: "He that is in you is greater than he that is in the world" (1 John 4:4 NKJV). That being said, should you find yourself being attacked, remember that you must be doing something right. You must be on the verge of giving the enemy a black eye. You must be on the threshold of your miracle. Keep the faith. You+God=victory.

I know that I tell you this all the time, but I will keep telling you this: Remember who you are and whom you belong to. You are a child of the Living God, and you belong to the Great I Am. You can do all things through Christ who strengthens you. You are blessed when you come in and go out. You are healed by His stripes. You are blessed to be a blessing. You are unstoppable. You are a child of the Living God. You are a King's kid. Hold your head up high and walk out your purpose and destiny.

"Having God on your side is a game-changer." ~ a Sherryism

> Lift up your hands in the sanctuary and praise the Lord. (Psalm 134:2 NIV)

I have it on good authority, warriors, that God wins. It is true that praise wins. Praise gets the Lord's attention. What better way to start your day than to have a song in your heart and praise on our lips.

"Our battles are won when the song is sung." ~ a Sherryism

If you have read my previous books, you know I really, really emphasize the *power of praise.* When you get up each morning, be determined to wash off yesterday's soil: the hurts, the sadness, the disappointments, and the bruises from life. Wash your face with the armor of praise.

We daily hear the noises of life all around us, but the Lord God, Creator of the universe, hears beyond the jibber jabber and listens to His children praising. Let it be you that He hears today. Let it be me. I want to get His attention. I need a victory. Praise wins.

Isaiah 61:3 reads, "He will bestow on them a crown of beauty instead of ashes the oil of joy instead of mourning, and a garment of praise instead of a spirit of despair" (NIV). I saw a quote from the 700 Club, which read, "I trust the next chapter because I know the Author." I love this.

Being an author myself, my readers are important to me. I want to bless you. I put in lots of midnight hours and research. I mix in laughs, tears, and encouragement. I didn't forget the yummy recipes. I have relationships with a lot of my readers. There is a bond of love, respect, and trust between us. When I begin to write, I don't always know how a chapter will look. But I do know that I always want the ending to be better than the beginning.

Much like not being able to live without God, I cannot write without God. He is my inspiration. He is my Editor in Chief. He is the Author of my life. So regardless of how the next chapter of my life begins, I will always trust because I know the Author. I know He loves me. We share a love and a bond. I know He will make sure the ending is better than the beginning.

As I say goodbye to you, I just want to tell you how much I love you. Always remember, you are loved. You are chosen. You are anointed. You are blessed. You are beautiful.

Please keep in touch with me. My website is at www.sherrymarieperguson.com. My Facebook page is Sherry Marie Perguson.

Shalom until we talk again.

Hugs and Blessings
Today, Tomorrow, Forever, and
Always, Sherry-Marie Perguson

Chapter 8

Warrior Recipes

A shared recipe in the South is more precious than gold ... and it always comes with a story.
—unknown

In this chapter, you will find an array of wonderful family tested and loved recipes from me, my family, and my friends.
I hope this becomes a chapter you refer to often and brings happiness to you and your family.
Bon appetit!
Remember that feeding the tummy is as important as feeding the soul.

Appetizers

You cannot have a Southern get-together, yu'all,
without loading the table with yummy nibbles.

It only takes a few because you
certainly don't want to ruin your
appetite for the main attractions!

Enjoy, yu'all!.

Artichoke Cream Cheese Dip

This is a much-loved recipe from my Bestie Donna Bach. Her daughter-in-law, Stephanie, makes this yummy dish, and the whole family loves it. She usually doubles the recipe.

1 can artichoke hearts, drained
1 (8-pounce) package cream cheese
1/2 cup mayonnaise (not fat free or light but the real thing)
1/2 cup Parmesan cheese (I use the shredded kind and add a lot more)
1 clove garlic

Preheat oven to 350 degrees F. Chop up artichokes. Mix everything together in large bowl. Place mixture in baking dish. Bake 20–25 minutes. It should be bubbly.

Deviled Eggs Dip

My little mama would cringe at the title of this recipe. She would never allow us to say her eggs had anything to do with the devil, so she called her deviled eggs, "dressed eggs."

12 eggs, hardboiled and shells removed
1/2 cup mayonnaise
4 ounces cream cheese, softened
2 tablespoons stone-ground mustard
1 tablespoon white wine vinegar
2 teaspoons chopped chives, divided
1/4 teaspoon garlic powder
Salt and black pepper to taste
1/4 teaspoon paprika for garnish

In a large bowl, mash eggs into an almost smooth consistency. Add mayonnaise, cream cheese, mustard, vinegar, and 1 teaspoon chopped chives. Season with garlic powder, salt, and pepper. Stir. Transfer into a pretty serving dish. Sprinkle with paprika and the remaining chopped chives right before serving. Serve with pita chips, tortilla chips, crackers, or anything else you want to use to dip.

Dill Pickle Dip

1 cup sour cream
4 ounces cream cheese
1 tablespoon minced onion
1/4 teaspoon salt
1 tablespoon fresh chopped parsley
1 tablespoon fresh dill
4 medium-size dill pickles, chopped

In a medium bowl, mix sour cream and cream cheese until smooth (You can use electric mixer). Stir in minced onion, salt, parsley, dill, and chopped dill pickles. Refrigerate until time to serve. Serve with chips or fresh veggies.

Recipe submitted by my Bestie Susan Horn.

Hawaiian Sliders Aloha

My family loves Hawaiian bread. We have to have it every get-together. We love all kinds of sliders, but this has to be one of my favorites. It's right up there with cheeseburger sliders.

Slider

1 package Hawaiian bread buns
4 ounces sliced deli ham
4 ounces mozzarella cheese slices
1 (16-ounce) can pineapple slices

Sauce

1/2 cup butter
1/2 teaspoon garlic powder

Slider

Preheat oven to 350 degrees F. Slice the Hawaiian bread buns lengthwise. In a 9x13-inch baking dish, place the bottom half of the buns. Place sliced ham on top of bun. Place slice of cheese on top of ham. Place pineapple slices on top of cheese. Place the top of the bun on top of the pineapple.

Sauce

Heat butter and garlic powder in a small saucepan until butter is melted. Use a pastry brush to brush melted mixture over the top of the buns.

Cover each slider with aluminum foil. Bake for 35–40 minutes.

Homemade Red Enchilada Sauce

How many times have you wanted to make enchiladas, looked in your pantry, and didn't have a can of sauce. Well, here is something I found in my mama's stash. It is really easy to make and tastes great. I didn't know exactly where to place this recipe in the book, so I decided to put it with the appetizers since it's not really a dish.

2 tablespoons extra-virgin olive oil
2 tablespoons flour
4 tablespoons chili powder
1/2 teaspoon onion powder
1/2 teaspoon garlic powder
1/2 teaspoon cumin
1/4 teaspoon salt
1 1/2–2 cups chicken broth

Heat the oil in a small pan over low to medium heat. Add flour and stir for about one minute. Add chili powder, onion powder, garlic powder, cumin, and salt. Stir. Gradually add the chicken broth, whisking the entire time (This prevents lumps).

Simmer for 15 minutes or until the enchilada sauce thickens. Stir often.

Use immediately or store in a mason jar in the refrigerator for up to one week.

Jalapeno Popper Wonton Cups

Wrappers

12 wonton wrappers

Filling

1 pound bacon, cooked and crumbled
1 cup shredded cheddar cheese
4 ounces cream cheese at room temperature
1/2 cup sour cream
4–5 jalapenos, washed, seeded, and chopped

Wrappers

Preheat oven to 350 degrees F. Spray12-cup muffin pan with nonstick cooking spray. Place one wonton wrapper in each muffin cup. Bake 8 minutes or until lightly browned. Remove from oven and let cool.

Filling

Separate and set aside a little bit of cooked bacon and cheddar cheese to use as topping. In a medium-size mixing bowl, mix rest of bacon and cheddar cheese. Mix in cream cheese, sour cream, and jalapenos. Stir well. Spoon mixture into wonton cups. Top each cup with rest of bacon and cheddar cheese. Return pan to oven and bake for 5-6 minutes or until cheese melts and wontons are a nice golden brown.

Pimento Cheese Spread

This recipe is submitted by my BFF, Jennifer Raskovich. Jen shares a sweet memory:

When we would visit our grandparents home in southern Indiana, Grandma always had a bowl of this pimento cheese in the fridge. She loved to cook. I have the recipe she wrote out for my mother almost sixty years ago. She made it with the old food grinder that attaches to the table. The recipe is exactly how she wrote it. She used mild cheese like longhorn or Colby. I have also made it with mild or sharp cheddar and have also found that either can be used, depending on your taste. Through trial and error, I learned that you must cook the egg mixture until it is very thick, otherwise the spread will be runny. If you have an old food grinder, use it. It seems to make a better spread than grating the cheese. It could be the nostalgia associated with it. Who knows?

Sauce

3 eggs
9 tablespoons sugar
6 tablespoons vinegar
dash of salt

Cheese and Pimento Mixture

1 lb. mild Longhorn cheese (shredded)
1 small jar whole pimentos (ground through food chopper)

Sauce

Mix eggs, sugar, vinegar, and salt. Then cook on low heat until it thickens. Remove from heat. Cool slightly.

Cheese and Pimento Mixture

Mix all ingredients by hand preferably, but you can use mixer. Do not beat it until smooth; you want to be able to see chunks of the cheese. Then add to sauce. Spread on whole-wheat or white bread to make sandwiches. It can also be a dip for your favorite chips and crackers.

Sausage Stuffing Bites and Cranberry Dip

Bites

1 pound ground Jimmy Dean sausage
1 stalk celery, finely chopped
1/2 cup finely chopped onions
1/2 teaspoon ground sage
salt and pepper to taste
1/2 cup shredded cheddar cheese
1/2 cup chopped dried cranberries
1 box stuffing mix, unprepared
2 eggs, beaten
1 cup chicken broth

Cranberry Dip

1 can whole berry cranberry sauce
1/4 cup orange juice
pinch of salt

Bites

Preheat oven to 375 degrees F. Line a 9x13-inch cookie sheet with parchment paper or wax paper.

In a large skillet, brown sausage over medium heat. Add celery, onions, sage, salt, and pepper. Cook until celery and onions are tender. Set aside and let cool for 10 minutes.

When cool, add cheese, cranberries, and stuffing. Stir mixture. Add eggs and chicken broth. Thoroughly stir until everything is well blended. With the palms of your hands, make individual bite-size balls and place on cookie sheet.

Bake for 15–20 minutes or until they become brown and toasty on top.

Cranberry Dip

In a medium saucepan, add cranberry sauce, orange juice, and salt. Stir until completely mixed together. Cook over medium heat until dip becomes thin but not too thin. Remove from heat and serve warm in a pretty serving dish.

Breakfast Delights

Starting your day off in style can be easy-peasy.

It will not only nourish you for your journey but will also delight and awaken your taste buds.

Breakfast Sausage Cake

2 cups cooked sausage (I use Jimmy Dean)
1 can grand-sized biscuits (8 biscuits)
12 eggs
2 cups frozen tater tots
2 cups shredded Mexican-blend cheese
1/4 cup milk
salt and pepper to taste

Preheat oven to 400 degrees F.

Brown sausage in skillet and then set aside.

Remove biscuits from can and cut into small cubes.

In a large bowl, beat the eggs with a whisk. Add the sausage, uncooked biscuit cubes, tater tots, cheese, and milk. Stir. Add salt and pepper. Place in medium-sized greased baking dish. Bake for 45 minutes.

Whcn donc, cut into squares. Serve while warm.

Buttermilk Pancakes

Recipe submitted by my beautiful longtime friend Marilyn Reynolds, who says that this is her family's favorite pancake recipe.

2 cups all-purpose flour
2 tablespoons sugar
2 teaspoons baking powder
1 teaspoon baking soda
1/8 teaspoon salt
2 eggs
1/2 teaspoon vanilla
2 cups buttermilk
6 tablespoons melted butter plus butter for griddle

In large bowl mix dry ingredients.

In another bowl whisk together the egg, vanilla, and buttermilk. Add wet ingredients to dry ingredients along with the melted butter. Stir until combined. Don't overmix (Will have some small lumps in it).

Heat griddle over medium heat. Lightly butter the griddle. Using 1/4 cup scoop, scoop batter and quickly pour onto hot griddle. When bubbles form on surface and bottom is golden brown, flip pancakes. Cook until they puff up and are brown on other side.

Cream Cheese Pancakes

1 1/4 cup all-purpose flour
1/2 teaspoon baking powder
1/2 teaspoon baking soda
1/4 teaspoon salt
2 large eggs (separate the egg yolks from the egg whites)
1 (8-ounce) package cream cheese
2/3 cup milk
1 tablespoon sugar
1 teaspoon vanilla
Oil for griddle

In a large bowl, combine flour, baking powder, baking soda, and salt.

In another bowl, whisk together egg whites until foamy.

In another bowl, beat cream cheese, egg yolks, milk, sugar, and vanilla.

Add the flour mixture to the cream cheese mixture. Stir until well blended but don't overmix. Stir in the egg whites.

Grease a large skillet or griddle with just enough oil to coat it. Heat the skillet or griddle. Pour 1/2 cup batter onto the griddle. Cook for 2 minutes or until bottom becomes golden brown. Flip over. Cook for another minute or until that side becomes golden brown.

Serve with butter and warm maple syrup or honey and fruit.

Hatch Green Chili Chicken Breakfast Casserole

Sauce

2–3 adobo peppers in sauce (1 small can), finely chopped
1 small can Hatch green chilies, drained and chopped
1 jar of Hatch Green Chile Sauce
2 cans of RO-TEL, drained (Use any heat or flavor, I prefer the chipotle)
2 tablespoons minced garlic
1 cup chopped onions
1/2 teaspoon cumin
1/2 teaspoon cilantro
1/2 teaspoon red pepper flakes
2 tablespoons organic chicken-flavored Better than Broth Paste
1/4 cup water

Casserole

12 eggs
1 large can whole roasted Hatch green chilies, sliced in halves and well drained
1 bag soft corn tortillas, sliced in halves
1 whole rotisserie chicken, shredded and mixed with 2 tablespoons of organic chicken-flavored Better Than Broth Paste and a sprinkle of Montreal Steak Seasoning
1 pound shredded cheese (mozzarella, pepper-jack, or Mexican blend)
Cotija cheese (to your taste), crumbled
sliced avocados (how many you prefer)

Preheat oven to 350 degrees F. Grease 9x13-inch casserole dish with coconut oil.

Sauce

Mix the adobo peppers, drained green chilies, Hatch Green Chili Sauce, RO-TEL, garlic, onions, cumin, cilantro, red pepper flakes, organic chicken-flavored Better than Broth Paste, and water. Set aside.

Whisk the eggs until they are a creamy yellow. Set aside.

Casserole

First pour a small amount of the RO-TEL and Hatch mixture into bottom of the casserole dish. Spread evenly. Next place half of the split green chilies in. Follow this with the corn tortillas, shredded chicken, shredded cheese, and then the sauce mixture. Repeat until all ingredients are used or casserole dish is full. Green chilies or corn tortillas can be the top layer. Pour the whisked eggs on top, making sure that it permeates sides and bottom of casserole. Sprinkle shredded cheese on top of this.

Bake for 30–45 minutes or until eggs set. Let stand for 5–10 minutes.

Top with crumbled Cojita cheese and sliced avocados. Cut into squares and serve garnished with salsa, pico de gallo, sour cream, or green onions and serve with warm, soft corn tortillas or tortilla chips.

Recipe submitted by my beautiful warrior girlfriend Cat Gillham.

Kentucky Hot Brown Quiche

1 (9-inch) frozen deep-dish pie crust
1 cup cooked and chopped turkey
1 cup shredded Swiss cheese
1/2 cup cooked and chopped bacon
1/2 cup diced tomatoes
3 eggs
1 cup heavy cream
3 tablespoons sour cream
salt and pepper

Preheat oven to 350 degrees F.

Spread turkey, cheese, bacon, and tomatoes in pie shell. Whisk eggs, heavy cream, and sour cream together. Add salt and pepper to taste. Pour egg mixture over the other ingredients in pie shell.

Bake 1 hour. Let quiche cool for 5 minutes before serving.

Spinach and Kale Quiche with Sweet Potato Crust

One year for our anniversary, my hubby reserved a weekend at a wonderful bed and breakfast in Prescott, Arizona. This is when and where I met Cat Gillham. She was the head chef there, and she served this fantastic quiche to us. It is the best and most unusual quiche that I have ever tasted. I love it.

Enough coconut oil to coat quiche dish and skillet
2 medium sweet potatoes, peeled and cut into 1/8-inch-thick slices, divided
coconut oil spray
1/2 cup finely chopped onion
1 (5-ounce) bag fresh baby spinach or a box of frozen spinach that has been thawed and the excess moisture has been drained from it
1 cup fresh finely chopped and deveined kale or a box of frozen kale that has been thawed and excess moisture has been drained from it
1/4 teaspoon kosher salt or sea salt

1/4 teaspoon freshly ground black pepper
1/4 teaspoon crushed red pepper flakes
8 eggs, whisked until a creamy yellow color (may add 2 teaspoons milk)
1 teaspoon finely chopped fresh rosemary
1 teaspoon fresh finely chopped thyme
1 tablespoon fresh minced garlic or garlic in a jar
1 cup grated cheese (use as much as you desire and use your favorite: pepper-jack, Gruyere, fontina, mozzarella, or my favorite, which is Trader Joe's five-cheese blend with asiago)
1 cup fresh chopped mushrooms
2 cups cooked and crumbled bacon or cooked sausage, drained

Preheat oven to 350 degrees F.

Grease deep-dish pie dish with coconut oil. Place all but a few of the sliced sweet potatoes in bottom of pie dish and up the sides, overlapping the slices slightly. Spray with coconut oil spray. Place in oven and bake for 10–15 minutes or until slightly softened. Remove from oven and let cool.

Spray skillet with coconut oil and saute spinach, kale, onion, mushrooms, and garlic just until the spinach and kale are wilted. Add rosemary, thyme, crushed red pepper, and salt and pepper to taste. Remove any moisture from the spinach and kale mixture.

Layer spinach mixture on the bottom of the cooled sweet potato crust. Then add cheese and a layer from the leftover sweet potato slices. Repeat this until all ingredients are used, ending with sweet potatoes. Pour beaten eggs over the quiche. You may have to move some of the filling from edges so that the eggs will permeate the entire quiche. Top with more cheese.

Cover with foil. Bake at 375 degrees F. for 20–30 minutes or until eggs set. Remove foil during last 10 minutes of baking. Let cool 15 minutes. Slice and serve.

Recipe submitted by my beautiful warrior girlfriend Cat Gillham.

Soups and Salads

There is nothing like a delicious, warm bowl of soup on a cold winter day, unless it is a cool, crisp salad on a hot summer day.

The soups and salads that I have shared are some of the best I have ever tasted.

Eat up my friends!

Bacon Broccoli Cashew Salad

1 pound bacon
2 pounds fresh broccoli
1/4 red onion
1 cup mayonnaise
1/2 cup white sugar
2 teaspoons cider vinegar
1 cup cashews

Fry the bacon until crispy. Then crumble it. Set it aside.

Cut broccoli into florets. Chop the piece of red onion finely.

In a large bowl, mix the mayonnaise, sugar, and vinegar. Mix together until sugar is dissolved (You can use a whisk). Add crumbled bacon, broccoli florets, onion, and cashews. Mix together until well coated.

Chill for 2–3 hours. Let stand at room temperature about 10 minutes before serving.

Bowtie Pasta and Spinach Salad with Chicken

I had a similar salad at Zupa's, came home, and decided to make my own version. This can easily be a meal in itself. Just add your favorite bread. I have also substituted shrimp for the chicken, and I love that version too.

8-ounce box of bowtie pasta
2 cooked chicken breasts, chopped
3 cups fresh spinach leaves
1 cup dried cranberries
3/4 cup cashews
1 (4-ounce) can mandarin oranges, drained
1/2 cup fresh chopped cilantro leaves
Ken's Steakhouse Lite Asian Sesame with Ginger and Soy Dressing

Cook pasta according to package instructions. Drain. Place cooked and drained pasta in a large bowl. Add chopped chicken, spinach leaves, cranberries, cashews, mandarin oranges, and chopped cilantro leaves. Toss until well blended. Drizzle Ken's Steakhouse Lite Asian Sesame with Ginger and Soy Dressing over the salad, toss again, and serve immediately.

Hot Bacon Dressing

My mama always made this incredible dressing. I looked for years in her stash of recipes and finally found it. I hope you will enjoy it.

3/4 pound bacon
1/2 cup brown sugar, packed
1/3 cup apple cider vinegar
1/3 cup of bacon drippings
1 1/2 tablespoons Dijon mustard
1 teaspoon cornstarch
1/4 cup vegetable oil
Sea salt and coarse black pepper to taste

In a skillet, cook bacon until crispy. Remove and place on paper towel. Set drippings aside. Crumble bacon. Place bacon in medium saucepan over low heat. Stir in sugar, apple cider vinegar, bacon drippings, and mustard. In a small bowl, dissolve cornstarch in 1 teaspoon cold water. Add to bacon mixture. Gradually add vegetable oil. Remove from heat. Add salt and pepper to taste.

Serve warm over baby spinach, sliced hardboiled eggs, sliced mushrooms, sliced cherry tomatoes, and sliced red onions.

Jerusalem Salad

I have seen and tasted several variations of this cucumber and tomato salad, but I love this one. The name alone makes me want to add it to my meal. My mama would always say that the USA was right in the middle of the name Jerusalem, and we should always be her friend.

Finely chopping the vegetables instead of a slicing chunky larger ones makes this almost like a salsa, but without the spice.

1 cup finely chopped cucumber
1 cup finely chopped tomato
1 cup finely chopped red onion
1 cup finely chopped flat-leaf parsley
2 tablespoons extra-virgin olive oil
1/2 teaspoon sea salt
1/2 teaspoon black pepper

Combine the cucumber, tomato, red onion, and parsley in a bowl. Drizzle olive oil over it. Sprinkle salt and pepper over it. Toss to mix well. Serve chilled.

Mama's Homemade Tomato Soup

We always had grilled cheese sandwiches with are tomato soup at mama's house. If you want a creamier soup, you can add some cream to the soup just before you take it off the heat. Stir the soup until the cream blends with the tomato mixture.

6 pieces of bacon
1 1/2 tablespoons tomato paste
1 tablespoon flour
1 teaspoon garlic powder
1 teaspoon onion flakes
1/2 teaspoon thyme
1 (28-ounce) can whole tomatoes
4 cups chicken broth

In a skillet, fry bacon until it is crispy. Remove and drain on paper towels. Chop into bite-size pieces.

In a large soup pot, stir together tomato paste and flour over medium heat. Add garlic powder, thyme, onion flakes, and thyme. Stir. Pour the tomatoes with their juice into a bowl and crush them. Add the crushed tomatoes, their juice, and the chicken broth to the soup pot. Simmer for 30 minutes. Stir frequently. If it doesn't thicken as desired, remove soup from pot, place in blender, and puree. Then return it back to the pot.

Sprinkle bacon over individual bowls and serve.

Posole

Recipe submitted by friend Carol Doppler, who says,

I like to use any cut of meat that has fat and bones and leaves both in the soup. Use what you like and even try it with chicken instead, but traditionally pork is used. I prefer the white hominy to the yellow because it's softer and looks prettier.

3 or more pounds cubed pork any cut (I use steaks or chops because half the work is already done)
1–2 large cans of white hominy, drained
1 white or yellow onion, roughly chopped or sliced (as in soups)
2 tablespoons chopped or crushed garlic
1 bay leaf
3 tablespoons ground cumin
2 tablespoons chili powder (Gebhardt is my preferred brand)
Salt and pepper to taste
3 cups finely shredded cabbage

Place all ingredients, except the cabbage, in a large soup pan and fill with water to 3 inches from the top. Bring to a boil, reduce to a simmer, cover, and cook until meat is tender. This usually takes about an hour or so. After first 20 minutes, taste broth periodically to adjust salt and pepper. If you desire, you can even add either a small can of hominy, a cubed potato, or 1/4 cup of rice.

When finished, garnish with sliced cabbage. Eat with rolled corn tortillas (optional of course).

Optional Garnishes

lemon wedges
sliced radishes
chopped onion
chopped cilantro
chopped jalapeno or serrano peppers
crushed chili flakes
fresh lemon or lime juice

Pumpkin Beef Stew

1/2 cup flour
3 pounds stew meat
3 tablespoons butter
1 cup chopped yellow onion
1/2 teaspoon garlic powder
4 cups beef broth or beef stock
2 cups pumpkin puree
1 tablespoon Worcestershire sauce
1 tablespoon sea salt
1 teaspoon black pepper
3 pounds potatoes, peeled and diced
1 pound carrots, peeled and sliced
3–4 thyme sprigs

Place the flour in a plastic bag. Place stew meat in bag. Shake until stew meat is completely covered with flour.

In a large soup pot, melt butter over medium heat. Brown the meat in the butter. Add onion, garlic powder, beef broth/stock, pumpkin puree, Worcestershire sauce, salt, and pepper. Stir well and bring to a boil. Reduce heat to low and simmer for 3 hours, stirring occasionally. After 3 hours, add potatoes, carrots, and thyme sprigs. Increase heat to medium and cook 30 more minutes.

When ready, serve with corn bread or biscuits.

Sherry-Marie's Easy Chicken Soup

1 large boneless chicken breast
1 small can cream of chicken soup
1 small can chicken broth
1 teaspoon Tuscan-style seasoning
1/2 teaspoon garlic powder
1/4 teaspoon ground black pepper
1 cup frozen green beans
1 cup frozen crinkle-cut carrots
1 cup frozen broccoli

Place all ingredients in crockpot, except the frozen veggies (green beans, carrots, broccoli).

Cook for 4 hours on low heat in Crock-Pot.

Then shred chicken while still in the Crock-Pot. Add frozen green beans, crinkle-cut carrots, and broccoli. Cook 30 minutes longer.

When done, serve hot with homemade corn bread, biscuits, or crackers.

Suddenly Salad on Steroids

I have seen several versions of this salad. This is my version. It's so yummy on a hot summer evening.

1 box Suddenly Salad red pepper flavor
1 cup chopped cucumber
1 cup chopped bell pepper
1 cup cubed longhorn cheese
1 can mexicorn, drained
1 can black beans, drained
1/4 teaspoon dill
1/4 teaspoon parsley

Make the Suddenly Salad as directed on the box, adding 3 tablespoons of extra oil and water. Stir in everything else. Chill at least one hour before serving.

Thanksgiving and Christmas Soup

Recipe submitted by warrior girlfriend Cat Gillham.

1 1/2–2 pounds ground organic turkey (can also use shredded chicken breast)
1 cup finely chopped onion
3 tablespoons minced garlic
2 tablespoons finely chopped fresh rosemary
2 tablespoons finely chopped fresh thyme
3–4 boxes organic chicken stock or broth
4 tablespoons Better than Broth organic chicken stock paste
6 large sweet potatoes, cooked and cubed
3 Yukon Gold potatoes, cooked and cubed
1 teaspoon ground turmeric
1 teaspoon ground sage
2 tablespoons pumpkin-pie spice
5 bay leaves (dried or fresh)
salt and pepper to taste
2 cans kidney beans, drained
2 cans black beans, drained
1 1/2–2 cups dried cranberries, divided

1 1/2 pounds kale, deveined and finely chopped (fresh or frozen)

2 large cans yams in syrup

1 can adobo peppers in sauce, several finely chopped (Set sauce aside)

1 tablespoon Montreal Steak Seasoning

1 batch honey sweet corn bread (baked and cut into squares)

You can buy the cornbread already made at your local grocery or make your favorite recipe.

Cook the ground turkey with the onion, minced garlic, rosemary, and thyme, until well done. Set aside.

In a very large stock pot, add the boxes of chicken stock, and chicken-stock paste. Bring to a boil and then reduce to simmer. Add cooked potatoes (sweet and gold). Add cooked turkey. Simmer 15 minutes. Add additional spices: turmeric, sage, pumpkin pie spice, bay leaves, Montreal Steak Seasoning, salt, and pepper to taste. Add beans (kidney and black). Add yams in syrup. Add adobo peppers. Add cranberries, saving a few for garnish, and chopped kale. Simmer at least 1 hour or longer.

When finished, ladle soup into bowls and add crumbled corn bread and extra cranberries.

Walt's Famous New York Potato Salad

Makes six servings.

Recipe submitted by my beautiful warrior girlfriend Deborah Donnelly, who tells this story,

This recipe belonged to my young ninety-five-year-old dad, Walter Reynolds. He was Irish, served in the navy, became a ceramic-tile setter, and loved to cook. We have been using this recipe for sixty plus years. It has been handed down from generation to generation. Whoever eats it always wants the recipe and for us to make it again.

Check out his picture in the photo gallery. Thanks Walt, you handsome man.

2 tablespoons bacon drippings
2 pounds of red potatoes, sliced
1/2 pounds lean, well-done bacon
2 celery stalks

3 scallionsShredded carrot (garnish on top of salad)
Green pepper, diced (optional)
1 tablespoon spicy mustard
1/2 teaspoon dried dill
Black pepper to taste
One cup Hellmann's Mayonnaise

Cut the potatoes into round slices. Cook in water until soft. Don't overcook. Cook bacon. Pour a little of the bacon drippings over sliced potatoes. Turn and mix well. Add all other ingredients, except mayonnaise and carrots and mix well. Then add mayonnaise. Garnish with carrots.

White Chicken Chili

1 pound boneless, skinless chicken breasts
1 (24-ounce) box of chicken broth
1 medium yellow onion, peeled and diced
2 cloves garlic, minced
2 (15-ounce) cans great northern beans, drained and rinsed
1 (15-ounce) can whole kernel corn
2 (4-ounce) cans diced mild green chilies
4 ounces cream cheese at room temperature
1/4 cup half-and-half
1 teaspoon sea salt
1 teaspoon cumin
3/4 teaspoon oregano
1/2 teaspoon coarse black pepper
1/2 teaspoon chili powder
1/4 teaspoon cayenne pepper

Place chicken breasts in bottom of Crock-Pot. Add all other ingredients. Stir slightly. Cook on low heat for 8 hours or on high heat for 4 hours.

Breads and Butters

If I have a weakness,

it is for homemade breads of all kinds.

I can make a whole meal out of
bread, butter, spreads, and tea.

I have chosen to share some of the favorites
that I have come across through the years.

I hope that you make each one of these.

When you do, make an extra loaf for me!

Alabama Pecan Bread

1 cup granulated white sugar
1 cup brown sugar
1 cup vegetable oil
4 large eggs, beaten
2 cups self-rising flour
1/4 teaspoon salt
1 teaspoon vanilla extract
2 cups finely chopped pecans

Preheat oven to 350 degrees F. Grease two 5x9-inch loaf pans with butter.

In a large bowl, stir together white sugar, brown sugar, oil, and beaten eggs. Stir in flour and salt. Add vanilla extract. Gently fold in pecans. Pour into greased loaf pans. Place in oven.

Bake 40–45 minutes or until toothpick inserted in middle comes out clean.

Apple Butter

8 medium red apples
2 tablespoons vanilla extract
1 1/2 cups brown sugar
4 teaspoons cinnamon
1 teaspoon ground cloves

Wash, core, and slice apples into fourths. Place in Crock-Pot. Add vanilla. Cook on low heat for 6 hours. Stir every couple of hours. When apples are tender and soft, mash with potato masher. Add brown sugar, cinnamon, and cloves. Cook on low heat for 5 more hours. Stir every hour or so.

When finished, spoon into small mason jars. Let them cool. Place lids on tightly.

Store in refrigerator. They keep for 3–4 weeks.

Banana Brownie Bread

2 very ripe bananas
1 box Betty Crocker Supreme Original Brownie Mix
1/2 cup butter, melted
3 eggs

Preheat oven to 350 degrees F. Grease bottom and sides of 5x9-inch loaf pan with cooking spray.

In medium bowl, mash bananas with a fork. Stir in brownie mix. Open chocolate syrup pouch (found in brownie mix) and pour it into the mixture. Add melted butter and eggs. Stir just until moistened. Pour into pan.

Bake 1 1/2 hours or until toothpick inserted in center comes out clean. Cool 10 minutes. Remove from pan to cooling rack. Cool completely.

Buttermilk Biscuits

This recipe was submitted by my beautiful friend Marilyn Reynolds. Marilyn tells me that her family dearly loves these biscuits.

2 cups all-purpose flour
2 teaspoons baking powder
1 teaspoon sugar
1/2 teaspoon baking soda
1/2 teaspoon salt
8 tablespoons cold butter cut into small cubes
3/4 cup cold buttermilk

Heat oven to 450 degrees F.

Mix dry ingredients. Cut butter into dry mixture until the size of very small peas. Add buttermilk and stir gently until dough forms a soft ball. (If too sticky to handle, add a bit more flour. If too dry to hold together, add a bit more buttermilk). Turn dough out onto floured surface. Do not knead but gently flatten and fold into thirds (like a letter) about five or six times. Roll to 1/2-inch thickness. Cut with 2-inch biscuit cutter. Place on baking sheet about 1 inch apart. Bake until golden brown or about 10 to 12 minutes.

Cat's Mexican Corn Bread Waffles

Recipe submitted by my beautiful warrior friend Cat Gillham, who tells me that she cooks up bacon, crumbles it, and freezes it so that she always has bacon crumbles to add to her recipes, which is a great idea.

It doesn't take long for the corn bread to get golden brown in the waffle maker. Sometimes, she cooks hers a little longer until they are crispy.

2 package Morrison's Texas Honey Sweet Corn bread Mix (You can also use the unsweetened mix)
1 small can Hatch chilies, drained
1 1/2 cups grated pepper-jack cheese or cheese of your preference
1 1/2 cups bacon crumbles
2 tablespoons salted butter, melted

In a large bowl, add all ingredients to the corn-bread mix. Stir until just blended.

Lightly spray your Belgian waffle maker with cooking oil. Turn on heat. When waffle maker is hot, spoon the batter onto it. Cook to desired consistency.

Enjoy with your favorite soup or chili.

These freeze great, and they are easy to heat up after frozen. You can either use a toaster, and oven, or a skillet.

Cranberry Butter

2 (12-ounce) bags of cranberries
1 cup packed brown sugar
1 cup apple cider
1 whole cinnamon stick

Place all ingredients in a small Crock-Pot. Stir well. Cook on high heat for 2 hours or until cranberries are soft. Remove the cinnamon stick. Let mixture cool. Pour the mixture into a blender and puree for 1 minute. Pour mixture through a strainer and back into the Crock-Pot. Cook uncovered on high heat for 2 more hours. Spoon the cranberry butter into small mason jars. Tightly close lids. When cool, store in refrigerator for up to 3 weeks.

Italian Garlic Butter

4 sticks salted butter at room temperature
2 tablespoons garlic paste
1/4 cup Parmesan cheese
1 tablespoon crushed parsley

Place butter in large mixing bowl of mixer and mix on low for 2 minutes. Add garlic paste, Parmesan cheese, and parsley. Beat 2 more minutes. Spoon into small mason jars. Tightly close lids. Store in refrigerator. Keeps as long as regular butter.

Maple Bacon Cheddar Biscuits

10 slices bacon, cooked to crispy, drained, and cut into small pieces
4 cups all-purpose flour
1 cup shredded mild cheddar cheese
4 teaspoons baking powder
1 teaspoon baking soda
1 1/2 teaspoons sea salt
3/4 cup and 2 tablespoons butter, melted and divided
1 1/2 cups buttermilk
6 tablespoons maple syrup, divided

Preheat oven to 450 degrees F. Grease a baking sheet or line it with wax paper.

In a large bowl, mix together bacon, flour, cheese, baking powder, baking soda, and salt. Stir in the 3/4 cup butter.

In a smaller bowl, whisk buttermilk and 4 tablespoons of maple syrup. Add this mixture to the flour mixture. Stir until it makes soft dough.

Place dough on a flat, floured surface. Knead 3–4 times. Roll out to 1 1/2-inch thickness. Cut out biscuits with cutter. Place on baking sheet.

Bake 15–20 minutes or until golden brown.

In a small bowl, mix 2 tablespoons melted butter and 2 tablespoons maple syrup. Remove biscuits from pan and brush the butter-syrup mixture over the top. Serve warm.

Monkey Butter

5 medium-ripe bananas (no brown spots)
1 (20-ounce) can crushed pineapple with juice
1/4 cup coconut milk
3 cups granulated sugar
3 tablespoons lemon juice from bottle or freshly squeezed

Peel and slice the bananas. Place in large pot. Add crushed pineapple with the juice, coconut, sugar, and lemon juice. Bring to a boil over medium heat, stirring constantly. Reduce to low heat and simmer until it thickens, stirring constantly. Spoon into small mason jars. Let cool. Place lids on tightly. Put in refrigerator.

Keep 4–6 weeks.

Pumpkin Butter

2 (15-ounce) cans pumpkin puree
1 cup sugar or maple syrup
1/2 cup apple cider
1/2 teaspoon ground cinnamon
1/2 teaspoon ground ginger
1/2 teaspoon ground nutmeg
1/2 teaspoon vanilla extract

Combine all ingredients and stir. Put in Crock-Pot. Cook on low heat for 1 hour. Stir. Cook 2 more hours, uncovered. Spoon the butter into small mason jars. Let cool. Place lids on tightly and put in refrigerator.

Use within 10 days.

Southern Sweet Potato Corn Bread

2cups cornmeal2 cups all-purpose flour
½ cup granulated sugar
2 ½ tablespoon baking powder
1 teaspoon ground cinnamon
1/2 teaspoon ground nutmeg
1½ teaspoons salt
½ 2 2/3 cups cooked and mashed sweet potatoes
4–5 pats butter
4 large eggs
3/4 cup buttermilk or whole milk
1/3 cup extra virgin olive oil

Preheat oven to 425 degrees F. Spray a large cast-iron skillet with cooking oil. Place in oven to heat.

In a large bowl, whisk cornmeal, flour,, sugar, baking powder, cinnamon, nutmeg, and salt.

In a separate bowl, whisk together eggs, milk, olive oil; gently stir in sweet potatoes a little at a time until evenly moistened.

Add the egg and milk mixture to the dry ingredient a little at a time.

Remove hot skillet from oven. Pour corn-bread mixture into skillet.

Bake 25–30 minutes or until golden brown and done in the center.

Remove from oven and immediately put several pats of butter on top so that they melt through the cracks on the top of the corn bread.

Zucchini Bread

4 cups flour
1 tablespoon baking soda
1/4 teaspoon salt
1 1/2 teaspoons cinnamon
1/4 teaspoon nutmeg
5 eggs
1 1/2 cups oil
2 cups white sugar
1 cup brown sugar
1 tablespoon vanilla
2 cups shredded zucchini
1 cup shredded apples (red preferred)
1 1/2 cups chopped walnuts

Preheat oven to 350 degrees F.

Combine first 5 ingredients and set aside.

Combine eggs, oil, sugars, and vanilla in a large bowl. Beat well approximately 2 minutes. With a spatula, fold in remaining ingredients. Add first five ingredients and stir just until moistened. Pour mixture into three prepared loaf pans. Sprinkle top of each loaf with powdered sugar.

Bake for 50–55 minutes or until a toothpick comes out clean.

Recipe submitted by my beautiful friend Carol Doppler.

The Sides

Veggies are no longer the boring
portion of our meals.

These recipes prove it!

Enjoy!

Bacon Cheese Fries

1 package (32-ounce) frozen French fries
1 cup shredded cheddar cheese
1/2 cup thinly sliced green onions
1/4 cup cooked bacon

Bake French fries according to package directions.

When baked, place fries on broiler-proof platter. Sprinkle with cheese, onions, and bacon. Broil for 1-2 minutes or until cheese is melted.

Serve with ranch dressing.

Recipe submitted by my beautiful Bestie Susan Horn.

Cider-Glazed Carrots
with Walnuts

2 ½ pounds medium-size carrots, peeled and cut into 2-inch diagonal pieces (makes about 9 cups)
1/4 cup packed light brown sugar
3 tablespoons apple cider vinegar
2 tablespoons unsalted butter
1 teaspoon kosher salt
1/2 teaspoon dry mustard
1/2 teaspoon paprika
1/2 cup toasted walnut pieces
1 tablespoon chopped fresh flat-leaf parsley

Place carrots in a large saucepan with water to cover all. Bring to a boil over high heat. Reduce heat to low and simmer until tender (about 3–5 minutes). Drain. Set aside.

Combine brown sugar, vinegar, butter, salt, mustard, and paprika in a large nonstick skillet. Cook over low heat, stirring often, until butter melts. Increase heat to medium high and bring to a boil. Reduce heat to medium. Add cooked carrots. Continue to cook, stirring constantly, until carrots are glazed and their sauce is syrupy (about 3–4 minutes). Stir in walnuts. Sprinkle with chopped parsley and toss to combine. Serve immediately.

Recipe submitted by my beautiful warrior girlfriend Carolyn Adair.

Corn Casserole

2 packages (12-ounce.) frozen corn, thawed and divided
2 large eggs
1/4 cup all-purpose flour
2 tablespoons sugar
2 tablespoons butter at room temperature
1/2 teaspoon garlic powder
1/2 teaspoon onion powder
1/4 teaspoon cayenne pepper
Salt and pepper to taste
1 cup grated sharp cheddar cheese, divided
1 cup grated Monterey jack cheese, divided
10 slices bacon, cooked, crumbled, and divided

Preheat oven to 350 degrees. Spray 9x13-inch baking dish with nonstick cooking spray.

In a large bowl, combine 1 package corn, eggs, flour, sugar, butter, garlic powder, onion powder, and cayenne pepper. Stir until mixed well. Add salt and pepper. Beat until mixture is nice and smooth. Stir in remaining 1 package of corn,

1/2 cup cheddar cheese, 1/2 cup Monterey jack cheese, and 7 pieces of bacon. Pour into baking dish. Spread out evenly. Top with remaining cheese and bacon.

Place in oven. Bake 25–30 minutes or until bubbly. Remove from oven. Serve hot.

Green Bean Fries

1 pound fresh green beans, washed, dried, and
ends trimmed off
1 tablespoon extra-virgin olive oil
1/2 cup grated Parmesan cheese
1/4 teaspoon sea salt
1/4 teaspoon coarse black pepper
1/4 teaspoon smoked paprika

Preheat oven to 425 degrees F. Place aluminum
foil on bottom of a 9x13-inch baking sheet. Spray
cooking spray on foil.

Put green beans in a medium-size bowl. Stir olive
oil into green beans, making sure all beans are
covered.

In another bowl, mix Parmesan cheese, sea salt,
black pepper, and smoked paprika.

Place a few green beans at a time, in the Parmesan
mixture and stir to coat. Place coated beans in a
single layer on the baking sheet.

Bake (or roast) for 10–12 minutes. Turn oven to broil and broil for about 2 minutes more or until beans begin to brown and crisp.

After removing from oven, serve hot with ranch dip.

Potato Cheese Puffs

This yummy and really easy recipe was comes from my Bestie Tari Nixon. She makes note that this is a good way to use up leftover mashed potatoes. She usually figures on one cup per person.

4 cups mashed potatoes
1 cup grated cheddar cheese
1/2 cup chopped onion
1 egg, beaten

Preheat oven to 350 degrees F.

Mix all ingredients in a bowl.

Place in baking dish.

Bake for 1 hour.

Red Cabbage and Apples

Recipe submitted by my beautiful warrior friend Deborah Donnelly, who tells us,

This is an old traditional Christmas Eve dish in many countries. My Irish father and German mother made sure we had this delicious vegetable on all holidays and especially Christmas.

2 tablespoons olive oil
1 small onion, finely sliced
1 pound red cabbage, finely shredded
One medium apple, cored and cut into half-inch chunks
2 tablespoons red wine vinegar
1 bay leaf
4 tablespoons of water
3 tablespoons sugar
Salt and pepper to taste

Warm olive oil in a deep, thick-bottomed pan. Add onion and cook until golden and translucent. Add cabbage, apple, vinegar, bay leaf, sugar and

4 tablespoons of water. Cook over moderate heat (It should simmer gently) for 20 minutes or so. Season with salt and freshly ground pepper. It is ready when tender but still has some bite when tasted.

Roasted Cabbage Wedges

1 cabbage
1 teaspoon sea salt
1 teaspoon coarse black pepper
2 tablespoons grated Parmesan cheese

Preheat oven to 425 degrees F.

Wash cabbage. Slice it into 1-inch or 2-inch wedges. Place sliced wedges on 9x13-inch baking sheet. Sprinkle sea salt, black pepper, and Parmesan cheese all over the top of it.

Bake for 30 minutes. Serve hot.

Roasted Parmesan Green Beans

1 pound fresh green beans
2 tablespoons PANKO
2 tablespoons grated Parmesan cheese
2 tablespoons extra-virgin olive oil
1/2 teaspoon sea salt
1/4 teaspoon garlic powder

Preheat oven to 400 degrees.

In a large bowl, place all ingredients in medium-size bowl. Toss to coat well. Spread green-bean mixture on a 9x13-inch baking sheet. Bake (roast) for 10 minutes. Take out of oven. Turn green beans over with a spatula. Place back in oven and bake (roast) for 10 more minutes.

Rutabagas

Recipe submitted by my beautiful warrior friend Deborah Donnelly, who explains,

This is an old recipe handed down by my parents, Walter and Theresa. They lived in New York and served this dish during all our holidays. When we invite our friends over now, they always look forward to this delicious vegetable.

2–3 pounds rutabagas
2 teaspoons salt, divided
1/3 cup butter
1/2 teaspoon ground black pepper

Peel rutabagas and cut into chunks. Put chunks in a large saucepan and cover with water. Add 1 teaspoon of salt. Bring to a boil. Reduce heat, cover, and simmer for 25–30 minutes or until tender. Drain and let them dry in colander. When dry, mash rutabagas and mix in butter, the remaining teaspoon of salt, and black pepper.

Tennessee Corn Bread Salad

My mom had this recipe in her stash. I love corn-bread salads. Another great one that my family has used for years is called "Southern Corn-Bread Salad." You can find the recipe in my book *Southern & Sassy ... with a Side of Faith.*

Makes 12 servings.

Dressing

1 cup mayonnaise
1/4 cup sweet pickle juice

Salad

3 cups baked and crumbled Krusteaz Southern Cornbread
12 slices bacon, cooked and crumbled
3 cups chopped tomatoes
1 cup chopped celery
1 cup chopped onions (I use green onions)
1/2 cup chopped sweet pickles

Dressing

Whisk together ingredients. Set aside.

Salad

Layer half of crumbled corn bread in large bowl.

Combine remaining salad ingredients. Spoon half of it over corn bread. Drizzle half of dressing salad layer. Repeat layers.

Chill 2–3 hours before serving.

Main Dishes
and Casseroles

This section features beef,
chicken, fish, and pork.

Your palate will thank me.

Angels on Horseback
(Oysters)

My mama loved her oysters and passed down that love to me and my sister. She really loved to make her own fried rolled oysters. I found this handwritten recipe in her stash, and it is fabulous. Seriously, if you love oysters and bacon, this recipe is a match made in heaven. Enjoy.

6 bacon slices
2 cans oysters or 12 fresh oysters
1 fresh lemon or bottled lemon juice
1–2 teaspoons cayenne pepper
2 tablespoons chopped parsley

Preheat oven to 400 degrees F.

Cook bacon to not quiet done stage. Cut each slice in half. Set aside.

Remove oysters from can and drain juice. Sprinkle oysters with lemon juice (to your taste). Sprinkle with cayenne pepper and parsley. Roll one half slice of bacon around each oyster. Secure with wooden toothpicks. Place on baking tray that has been lined with wax paper.

Bake 5–10 minutes or until bacon is cooked and oysters are hot and bubbly.

Serve hot with spicy hot ketchup or cocktail sauce.

Brown Sugar Garlic Chicken

5 boneless, skinless chicken thighs
2 tablespoons minced garlic
1/2 teaspoon sea salt
1/4 teaspoon coarse black pepper
1/2 cup packed brown sugar

Place chicken, garlic, salt, and pepper in a Crock-Pot. Stir until chicken is well coated. Sprinkle brown sugar over all the chicken.

Cook on low heat in Crock-Pot for 7–8 hours (or 4 hours on high heat).

Cheesy, Beefy, Bacon Tater Tot Casserole

1 pound lean ground beef (or you can use 1 pound cooked and shredded chicken)
1 onion, chopped
2 cups shredded sharp cheddar cheese
8 slices bacon, cooked crispy and crumbled
4 cups frozen tater tots

Preheat oven to 400 degrees F. Spray a 9x9-inch baking dish with nonstick cooking spray.

In a skillet, cook ground beef and onion until beef is brown. Drain excess fat. If using chicken, just add onion to the cooked and shredded chicken. Place in the baking dish. Add cheddar cheese, bacon, and tater tots.

Bake 30–35 minutes or until tater tots are golden brown and casserole is completely heated.

Chicken Doritos Bake

One night I found myself with a chicken breast to cook, but I was tired of the same old, same old. So I looked in the pantry and the fridge to find something wonderful and came up with this. My hubby loves it. Enjoy.

4 boneless, skinless chicken breasts
1/2 teaspoon garlic
salt and pepper to taste
4–6 cups crushed Doritos (original flavor)
1 cup La Victoria Green Taco Sauce
1 pound Mexican-blend shredded cheese

Preheat oven to 375 degrees F.

In an oven-safe dish, layer everything exactly as listed.

Bake 45–50 minutes or until chicken is completely done and tender and sauce and cheese are bubbly.

Chicken Enchiladas
with Green Sauce

1 small can diced green chilies
3 pounds cooked, shredded boneless chicken
1 dozen flour tortillas
1 (8-ounce.) package cream cheese
2 large packagesshredded Monterey-jack cheese
Green enchilada sauce

Preheat oven to 375 degrees F.

Mix can of chilies with the chicken. Set aside.

Spread tortillas with a 1-inch wide line of cream cheese right down the middle (approximately 1 healthy tablespoon). Spoon equal amounts of chicken on top of cream cheese in each tortilla. Sprinkle each with shredded cheese, roll up, and place in 9x13-inch baking dish, cozied next to each other. Pour green sauce over the entire pan but do not completely submerge enchiladas, or they'll be too soggy. Cover with shredded cheese. Be as generous as you like.

Bake 30 minutes or until cheese is melted and slightly bubbly.

Additional notes

I like chicken breasts or thighs. I usually boil the meat or cook it in the Crock-Pot with garlic powder, chopped onions, salt, white pepper, cumin, or anything else you might put on your taco meat. You can also make this really easy by using a whole deli chicken.

Don't like green sauce?

Try using this sauce as a substitute (kids and crowds love this version)

a large can of cream-of-chicken soup
3–5 pounds fresh tomatillos
2 whole medium onions
1 large head of fresh garlic cloves, peeled

Steam all ingredients in a vegetable steamer.

When tender, liquefy it in a blender. Add salt to taste.

Recipe submitted by my friend Carol Doppler.

Chicken Noodle Chops

2 cups Shake 'n Bake
3–4 boneless pork chops
1 can chicken noodle soup

Preheat oven to 350 degrees F.

Pour Shake n' Bake into a ziplock baggie. One at a time, place pork chops in the baggie and shake well to coat the chops evenly. Place the coated pork chops in a baking dish. Pour the chicken noodle soup over the pork chops.

Bake 30–40 minutes.

Recipe submitted by my Bestie Tari Nixon.

Chicken Yogurt Thyme Salad on Croissants

Several years ago, my husband was admitted to the hospital. While I was staying with him, I wandered down to the café. I found some of the best chicken salad that I had ever tasted. Wonder of wonders, the package listed all the ingredients in it. I came home, and through trial and error, came up with this recipe that is close to the chicken salad I so enjoyed from the hospital café. I picked up the chicken breast from the deli at my local grocery store.

2 green onions, finely chopped
1/2 celery stalk, finely chopped
1 tablespoon Greek yogurt
1 tablespoon mayonnaise
1 teaspoon Dijon mustard
1 teaspoon finely chopped fresh thyme
1/8 teaspoon lemon juice
salt and pepper to taste
2 boneless, skinless chicken breasts, cooked

In a medium bowl, mix all ingredients until well combined. Cut the chicken breast into small pieces and add to yogurt mixture. Serve on a croissant.

Chili Dog Casserole

2 cans (15-ounce) chili with beans, divided
1 package (16-ounce) beef hot dogs
10 (8-inch) flour tortillas
1 (8-ounce) package shredded cheddar cheese

Preheat oven to 425 degrees F.

Spread one can of chili over the bottom of a 9x13-inch baking dish. Roll up hot dogs inside the tortillas. Place in the baking dish and on top of the chili. After all the hot dogs are in the dish, spread the second can of chili over the top of them. Sprinkle cheese evenly over the top.

Cover the baking dish with aluminum foil. Bake 30 minutes.

Fiesta Lime Chicken
and Rice Bowl

1 package Spanish rice
1 1/4 pound chicken breast, cut into bite-size
pieces
1 teaspoon chili powder
1 tablespoon cooking oil
1 tablespoon lime juice
Your favorite taco toppings

Cook the Spanish rice according to package. Set
aside.

Sprinkle chicken with chili powder. In large
nonstick skillet, heat 1 tablespoon cooking oil
over medium to high heat. Add the chicken and
cook until thoroughly done (about 5 minutes),
stirring occasionally. Stir in lime juice. Add
all ingredients to the Spanish rice in a serving
bowl. Top with your favorite taco toppings. Serve
immediately.

Topping Suggestions

Shredded cheddar cheese, chopped tomatoes, chopped onion, and crumbled tortilla chips

Recipe submitted by warrior girlfriend Carolyn Adair.

Fifties-Style Salisbury Steak

1–2 cans cream of mushroom soup, divided
1 pound ground beef
1/3 cup dry breadcrumbs
1/2 cup chopped onion
1 egg, beaten
2 teaspoons chopped fresh parsley
1 teaspoon garlic powder
1/2 teaspoon black pepper
1 1/2 cups sliced mushrooms or 1 (8-ounce) can sliced mushrooms

In a large bowl, mix 1/4 cup of the soup, ground beef, breadcrumbs, onion, egg, parsley, garlic powder, and pepper. Shape into firm patties. Brown patties in a skillet. Mix together the mushrooms and remaining soup. Add to the skillet. Reduce heat to low. Cover. Cook for 20 minutes or until the patties are thoroughly cooked, turning them occasionally.

Recipe submitted by my Bestie Susan Horn.

Jimmy Buffet's Cheeseburger in Paradise

1 pound lean ground beef
1 large onion, chopped
1/2 teaspoon of garlic powder
1/2 teaspoon of seasoned salt
dash of Worcestershire sauce
1 cup shredded cheddar cheese
1/4 cup shredded mozzarella cheese
1 cup milk
2 eggs
1/2 cup Bisquick mix

Preheat oven to 400 degrees F. Spray a 9-inch pie pan with cooking spray.

In a skillet over medium heat, brown beef. Add onion. Drain excess fat. Add garlic powder, salt, and Worcestershire sauce. Spread ground beef mixture into the prepared pie pan. Sprinkle with the shredded cheeses.

In a small bowl, mix together milk, eggs, and Bisquick mix, removing all lumps. Pour over the layer of shredded cheese.

Bake for 25 minutes or until a knife comes out clean.

Laurita's Cabbage Rolls

This is my sister Laurita's recipe. She says there is no need for fillers like rice or breadcrumbs, unless you just want them.

1 pound ground turkey
1/2 cup chopped onions
1 cup crumbled thick bacon
1/4 teaspoon salt
1/4 teaspoon black pepper
1 small can tomato sauce
12–15 large cabbage leaves

Preheat oven to 350 degrees F.

Cook and brown the ground turkey with the onions, bacon, salt, and pepper in a large skillet. Once browned, add tomato sauce.

Boil cabbage leaves just until pliable. Remove cabbage leaves from water. Pat with paper towel.

Spoon some turkey mixture into each cabbage leaf. Roll each leaf up and place in 9x13-inch baking pan.

Put in oven. Bake 30 minutes.

Mississippi Pot Roast

I love cooking in my Crock-Pot. This recipe is one of the best pot roasts I have ever made.

smidge of cooking oil
1 beef roast
1 package dry onion soup mix
1 package dry ranch dressing mix
1 stick butter
7–8 whole pepperoncini

Pour just enough cooking oil to slightly grease the bottom of a Crock-Pot. Place roast into Crock-Pot. Sprinkle soup mix over roast. Sprinkle ranch dressing mix over soup mix. Place one stick of butter on top of the mixes. Place the whole pepperoncini all around the top of the roast.

Cook roast overnight on low heat or for 4–5 hours on high heat during the day.

My Mama's Goulash

It seems like Mama made this at least once a week, always with corn bread or homemade biscuits. It was heavy on the Italian seasoning. Bless her heart.

1 pound lean ground beef
1 can red beans
1 can pinto beans
2 cans diced tomatoes
1 medium onion, chopped
2 cloves garlic, minced
3 cups tomato sauce
2 cups water
1 cup beef broth
3 teaspoons Worcestershire sauce
1 teaspoon Italian seasoning
1 1/2 teaspoons chili powder
salt and pepper to taste
3 cups cooked elbow macaroni

In a skillet, brown the ground beef. Remove skillet from heat. Drain meat, remove from skillet, and place in a large soup pot. Add red beans, pinto beans, diced tomatoes, onion, garlic, tomato sauce, water, beef broth, Worcestershire sauce, Italian seasoning, chili powder, salt, and pepper. Cook on medium high heat about 20 minutes. Stir occasionally.

Meanwhile, cook the elbow macaroni per instructions on the package. When the macaroni is cooked, add to the soup pot mixture. Reduce heat and simmer for 10 minutes.

Orange Chicken

1 (12-ounce) jar orange marmalade
1/2 cup packed brown sugar
1/4 cup soy sauce
2 tablespoons chili sauce
1 teaspoon salt
1 (3–4 pound) whole chicken
1/4 cup cornstarch
1/4 cup orange juice
1 fresh orange
2 tablespoons chopped fresh cilantro leaves

In a small bowl, mix marmalade, brown sugar, soy sauce, chili sauce, and salt. Place chicken in the Crock-Pot breast side down. Pour marmalade mixture all over the chicken. Place cover on the Crock-Pot and cook on low heat for 4–5 hours.

When finished, remove chicken and place on cutting board. Let stand about 10 minutes. Then cut into bite-size pieces. Set aside.

In a small bowl, mix cornstarch and orange juice. Stir this into the liquid that was left in the Crock-Pot. Cover. Cook on high heat for 15 minutes or until the sauce thickens.

While this is cooking, line a large, rimmed sheet pan with foil and place the chicken on the pan. Cut the orange into 6–8 slices. Place these around the chicken. When sauce in the Crock-pot is ready, brush the chicken and the oranges with it. Place chicken in oven and broil 4–5 minutes or until skin is nice, brown, and crisp. Sprinkle with cilantro. Serve over white or brown rice.

Pickle Biscuits with Ham

2 1/2 cups self-rising flour
1/2 cup (1 stick) butter
4 tablespoons dill pickle relish, drained
1 cup buttermilk
mustard
1 pound Hormel brown sugar ham, sliced

Preheat oven to 475 degrees F. Grease or place wax paper or parchment paper on cookie sheet.

In a large bowl, mix flour and butter.

In a smaller bowl, mix relish and buttermilk together.

Add buttermilk mixture to flour mixture. Stir really well to combine everything. Dough will be a little sticky. Place dough onto lightly floured board or smooth surface. Lightly sprinkle flour over dough. With a lightly floured rolling pin, roll dough into a 3/4-inch thickness. Fold the dough in half. Repeat the rolling process 3 more times.

Then cut into biscuits using a floured 2 1/2 inch round biscuit cutter. Reshape the scraps every time and roll out to 3/4-inch thickness, Cut with biscuit cutter until all the dough is used.

Bake for 15–20 minutes or until lightly brown. Remove from oven.

When finished, brush with melted butter and slice. Lightly spread mustard on bottom slice. Add 1–2 pieces of ham. Place top of biscuit on ham. Enjoy.

Root Beer Pork BBQ

1 tablespoon pink Himalayan salt
1 tablespoon chili powder
2 pound boneless pork shoulder roast
1 (12-ounce) bottle of root beer
1 (16-ounce) bottle of BBQ sauce (use your favorite), divided
1 teaspoon Worcestershire sauce
1 package (8-count) hamburger buns

Rub the salt and chili powder all over the roast. Mix root beer, 1 cup of BBQ sauce, and Worcestershire sauce. Place sauce in Crock-Pot. Add the roast. Cook on low heat 6–7 hours.

When finished, shred the pork into strips. Remove any fatty pieces. Add the rest of the BBQ sauce. Stir. Cook 30–40 more minutes.

When done, serve hot on buns.

Rotisserie Style Chicken

2 tablespoons packed brown sugar
2 teaspoons chili powder
2 teaspoons salt
1 teaspoon black pepper
1 whole chicken (3–4 pounds)

Spray a 5-quart oval Crock-Pot with cooking spray.

In a small bowl, mix together brown sugar, chili powder, salt, and pepper.

Using paper towels, pat chicken dry, both the inside and outside. Rub chicken all over with the sugar and spice mixture. Place breast side up in the Crock-Pot. Cover and cook on high heat for 3 hours.

When finished, remove chicken from Crock-Pot. Let stand 15 minutes. Serve with your favorite veggies.

Sherry-Marie's Salmon Burgers

1 pound cooked salmon or 1 (16-ounce) can of salmon
2 eggs
3/4 cup breadcrumbs
1 teaspoon chopped chives
1 teaspoon parsley
1/2 teaspoon garlic powder
1/2 teaspoon cayenne pepper
1 teaspoon olive oil
1 teaspoon lemon juice
sprinkle of dill

Separate the salmon into small flakes. Mix eggs, breadcrumbs, chives, parsley, garlic powder, and cayenne together with the salmon. Form into hamburger-size patties. Heat olive oil in large skillet. Place burgers in the hot oil and fry until golden brown and crispy, just a few minutes on each side. Remove from skillet. Place on paper towel to drain. After done draining, sprinkle each patty with lemon juice. Sprinkle dill on each patty.

Serve with your favorite bun and chips or as a main entree with a veggie and salad (whichever you prefer).

Sherry-Marie's Sweet and Sassy Pork Chops

I cook pork chops a lot (several times a week). I'm always trying to up my game on homemade recipes. This one is my very favorite one, I think you will enjoy it.

2 butterfly-cut boneless pork chops
4 slices Muenster cheese
2 red apples
1 teaspoon cinnamon
1/2 teaspoon sugar

Preheat oven to 350 degrees F. Spray casserole dish with olive oil spray, just coating bottom. Place pork chops in casserole dish. Place 2 slices of cheese on top of each pork chop. Slice apples in half from top to bottom. Then slice each half in half again, from top to bottom. Layer half the slices from apples on top of each pork chop. Sprinkle cinnamon and sugar over the apples. Bake 45 minutes.

Sherry-Marie's Tuscany Chicken

When eating, take a whole cherry tomato with each bite of chicken. The explosion of flavor is oh so yummy.

2 skinless, boneless chicken breasts
a couple shakes of garlic powder
a couple shakes of smoked paprika
a couple shakes of chopped cilantro leaves
½ - 1 teaspoon salsa fiesta seasoning or Italian seasoning (depending on your taste)
18 cherry tomatoes, whole
1/2 cup chopped onions
1/2 cup chopped bell peppers
2 pat of butters

Preheat oven 350 degrees F. Spray baking dish with olive oil spray.

Place chicken in baking dish. Sprinkle garlic powder, smoked paprika, and chopped cilantro leaves over chicken. Cover chicken completely with salsa fiesta seasoning. Place whole cherry tomatoes all around the chicken. Sprinkle chopped onions and chopped bell peppers all over the chicken. Place one pat of butter on top of each chicken breast.

Cook 45–50 minutes.

Shrimp Boil

4 tablespoons butter, melted and divided
1 1/2 teaspoons Cajun or Old Bay seasoning, divided
1 pound small new potatoes
1 (14-ounce) package kielbasa sausage
1 pound extra-large shrimp, uncooked, deveined, and peeled, but leave the tails on
6–8 frozen mini corn on the cob
1/4 cup chopped fresh parsley leaves
1 lemon, thinly sliced

Preheat oven to 425 degrees F. Spray a 13x18-inch rimmed sheet pan with cooking spray.

Cut kielbasa into 1/2-inch slices.

Wash and quarter potatoes.

In a large bowl, mix 2 tablespoons of butter and 1/2 teaspoon of Cajun seasoning. Add potatoes. Stir to coat potatoes well. Place potatoes skin sides down in a single layer on the sheet pan.

Roast 20–22 minutes or until the potatoes are really tender. Remove from oven. Add kielbasa to the potatoes and stir.

In a large bowl, mix the remaining butter and Cajun seasoning (You can use the same bowl that the potatoes were in). Add shrimp. Stir to coat shrimp well.

Place shrimp and corn in the pan next to the potatoes and sausage. Keep everything in a single layer. Sprinkle with parsley leaves. Roast 8–10 minutes or until the shrimp are pink and cooked completely through and potatoes are brown and tender. Remove from oven. Stir to mix everything really well. Top with lemon slices and serve.

Southern Spicy
Buttermilk Chicken

4–5 boneless, skinless chicken breasts or thighs
(or 6–8 skinless chicken legs)
salt and pepper to taste
2 cups buttermilk (*must* be buttermilk)
1/4 cup Louisiana Hot Sauce
4 large eggs
1–2 cups self-rising flour

Sprinkle chicken with salt and pepper.

In a bowl, mix buttermilk, hot sauce, and eggs. Add chicken. Marinate in refrigerator overnight.

The next day, drain chicken. Place flour in ziplock baggie. Place one piece of chicken at a time in baggie. Shake until piece is coated with flour. Place the coated chicken pieces in skillet with hot oil. Fry chicken about 15 minutes on each side and until golden brown.

Sweet Tea and Buttermilk Chicken

2 cups buttermilk
2 cups sweet tea
1 teaspoon salt
2–3 boneless, skinless chicken breasts
4 tablespoons butter
1/3 cup vegetable oil
2 cups flour
dash of garlic powder
salt and pepper to taste

Stir together buttermilk, sweet tea, and salt. Place chicken in bowl. Pour mixture over chicken and marinate all day or overnight.

When ready to cook, heat oven to 425 degrees F. Heat a cast-iron skillet in the oven for 10 minutes. Remove skillet and add butter and oil. Place skillet back in the heated oven (to keep it hot).

Mix flour, garlic powder, salt, and pepper. Place half the flour mixture in a baggie, add the chicken one piece at a time, and shake vigorously until well coated. Place back in the buttermilk mixture. Add remaining flour to baggie for second coating. Place chicken in baggie again and coat well. Place chicken in the hot skillet (Be careful. Chicken may sizzle). Place skillet back in the oven and bake for 20 minutes. After 20 minutes, take the skillet out of the oven and flip the chicken. Place skillet back in the oven and cook another 20 minutes.

When finished, immediately remove from skillet and serve.

Sweet Tea Ribs

1 1/2 pounds beef ribs
1/2 package McCormick Smokin' Sweet Tea Marinade
1 tablespoon extra-virgin olive oil
1 tablespoon honey
2 medium potatoes with skins
Salt and pepper to taste

Wash meat. Place in a ziplock baggie. Add marinade, olive oil, and honey. Seal and refrigerate overnight (or at least 2 hours).

When meat is ready, wash potatoes. Prick holes all over potatoes and rub with olive oil. Sprinkle with salt and pepper. Place in Crock-Pot. Add meat and spread it out. Pour the juices left in the baggie into the Crock-Pot. Cook on low heat for 4 hours. Don't overcook.

Taco Casserole

2 pounds ground beef (or ground turkey)
salt and pepper to taste
2 packages taco seasoning
4 large eggs
3/4 cup milk
1 1/4 cups Bisquick baking mix
1/2 cup sour cream
2 cups finely shredded lettuce
2 cups finely chopped tomatoes
1 cup sliced black olives
2 cups shredded cheddar cheese

Preheat oven to 400 degrees F. Spray 9x13-inch casserole dish with cooking spray.

In a skillet, cook beef until brown. Salt and pepper to taste. Drain. Add taco seasoning (Prepare per package and remember to double the water since you are using 2 packages). Place meat in the casserole dish.

In a large bowl, beat eggs and milk together. Stir in Bisquick until combined well. Pour over meat. Put casserole dish in oven and bake for about 25–30 minutes or until Bisquick layer is a nice golden brown.

Let cool for a few minutes. Then spread sour cream over the Bisquick layer. Top with shredded lettuce, chopped tomatoes, sliced black olives, and shredded cheddar cheese. Serve immediately.

Taco Pizza

Recipe submitted by my beautiful warrior girlfriend Carolyn Thompson, who says,

I came up with this recipe off the top of my head. My kids, grandkids, and great-grandkids love it.

1 prepared pizza crust (size of your choice)
1–2 cups salsa, divided
1 pound hamburger meat
Couple dashes garlic powder
Couple dashes chili powder
(or 1 package taco seasoning)
shredded lettuce
chopped tomatoes
shredded cheese
(any other taco toppings you like)
Roll out pizza crust onto cookie sheet. Put a little bit of salsa on it. Bake as directed.

Meanwhile, cook hamburger with garlic powder, chili powder or taco seasoning, like you do for tacos.

Remove crust from oven and spread meat over top. Pile on shredded lettuce, chopped tomatoes, cheese, or any other taco topping). Cut in squares and don't forget to pass out the rest of the salsa.

Taco Spaghetti

1 (8-ounce) package Velveeta cheese
8 ounces of dry spaghetti
1 pound lean ground beef (or ground turkey)
1 (1-ounce) package taco seasoning
2/3 cup water
1 (10.75-ounce) can cream of chicken soup
1 (10-ounce) can ROT-EL diced tomatoes with green chilies
2 cups shredded cheddar cheese

Preheat oven to 350 degrees F. Spray a 9x9-inch casserole dish with cooking spray.

Cut Velveeta cheese into cubes. Set aside.

Cook spaghetti according to directions on package. Drain.

In a large skillet, cook the ground meat over medium heat until good and brown. Drain excess grease. Place the meat back into the skillet. Add taco seasoning and water. Stir and cook for 5 minutes. Then stir in cream of chicken soup, ROT-EL, and Velveeta cheese cubes. Reduce heat to low, stirring until cheese melts. Sir in cooked spaghetti, until everything is well blended. Pour into the casserole dish. Top with shredded cheddar cheese. Place in oven and bake for 30 minutes.

True Southern Ham, Green Beans, and Taters

2 pounds ham (or ham hocks if you prefer)
4 potatoes
2 pounds fresh green beans
3 cups chicken broth
black coarse ground pepper to taste

Dice the ham, potatoes, and onions. Place in Crock-Pot. Add green beans. Cover with chicken broth. Sprinkle pepper to taste. Cook on low heat for 6 hours.

Tuna Stuffed Avocados

My sister told me that eating avocados helps bring down your cholesterol, so I try to eat as many as possible. I love adding tuna salad to them. Enjoy.

1–2 avocados
1 (4.5-ounce) can tuna, drained
1/4 cup finely chopped green onions
1/4 cup diced red bell peppers
1/4 cup chopped cilantro leaves
1 tablespoon diced jalapeno
1 tablespoon lime juice
salt and pepper to taste

Cut the avocados in half. Remove pit. Scoop out a little of the avocado to widen the bowl area. Place the avocado you scooped out into a medium-size mixing bowl and smash. Add tuna, green onion, bell pepper, cilantro, jalapeno, lime juice, salt, and pepper. Stir until well mixed. Spoon the avocado mixture into the halved avocados. Enjoy.

Decadent Desserts

In the South, your meal is not complete
until dessert is served and savored.

I hope that I have served you an
abundance of goodies.

Enjoy to your heart's content!

Apple Pie Enchiladas

Sauce

1/2 cup butter
1/2 cup white sugar
1/2 cup brown sugar
1/2 cup water
1/2 teaspoon vanilla

Filling

1 (21-ounce) can apple pie filling
sauce, divided

Enchilada

6 (8-inch) whole-wheat tortillas

Filling

1 teaspoon cinnamon

Preheat oven to 350 degrees F.

Sauce

In saucepan over medium heat, combine butter, white sugar, brown sugar, and water. Bring to a boil, stirring constantly. Reduce heat and simmer 3 minutes.

Filling

Mix all filling ingredients together and set aside.

Enchilada

Spoon 1/4 cup filling evenly down center of each tortilla. Sprinkle with cinnamon. Roll up, tucking in edges. Place seam side down in dish coated with butter. Pour remaining filling over it and let sit 30 minutes.

Bake for 20 minutes or until golden brown. Serve hot with a scoop of ice cream and enjoy.

Recipe submitted by my beautiful warrior girlfriend Carolyn Thompson.

Are You Kidding Me? Cake

This has got to be the easiest cake ever. There are only three ingredients and no water. It's a moist cake, so you don't even need icing. But if you want to make a light sugar glaze to pour over it, that would be even yummier. There are a zillion ways to make different flavors by using different cake mixes with different pie fillings like

- ✧ Carrot cake mix with apple pie filling
- ✧ Chocolate cake mix with cherry pie filling
- ✧ Strawberry cake mix with strawberry pie filling
- ✧ Yellow cake mix with blackberry or blueberry filling
- ✧ Confetti cake mix with peach pie filling

You get the idea?

1 box yellow cake mix
3 large eggs, beaten
1 can pie filling (any flavor)

Preheat oven to 350 degrees F. Grease 9x13-inch baking pan with butter.

In a medium-size bowl, put in the cake mix, eggs, and pie filling. Stir until mixed well. Pour into greased baking pan.

Bake 35 minutes.

Best Southern Pie

1 3/4 cup sugar
1/2 cup buttermilk
1 stick of butter
3 tablespoons flour
1 teaspoon vanilla
couple shakes nutmeg
pinch of salt
1 (9-inch) pie shell, unbaked

Preheat oven to 400 degrees F.

Mix everything together. Pour into an unbaked 9-inch pie shell. Sprinkle the top with nutmeg.

Bake 15 minutes. Reduce oven to 350 degrees. Bake 45 minutes.

When finished, cool and let filling set. Then serve.

Cherry Chocolate Cake

Recipe submitted by my beautiful warrior girlfriend Carolyn Adair, who says that this is one of her favorite go-to desserts.

1 box chocolate cake mix
1 container cream cheese frosting
1 can of sweet cherry pie filling

Preheat oven to 350 degrees F.

Fix and bake the chocolate cake mix as directed on box. Let cool. When cool, cover entire cake with cream cheese frosting. Then spread cherry pie filling over cream cheese frosting.

It's ready to eat. Enjoy.

marshmallow crème is melted completely into the chocolate. Pour into prepared pans and let cool. Cut into squares.

Recipe submitted by my beautiful BFF Jennifer Raskovich.

Chocolate Marshmallow Pie

This recipe was lovingly shared by my beautiful warrior girlfriend Linda Grossman. She told me that this was her mom's recipe. It is Linda's favorite. She told me. "It's the bomb."

1/3 cup milk
4 Hershey chocolate bars with almonds
16 large marshmallows
1/2 pint whipping cream
1 premade pie crust, baked

Put milk and Hershey bars in double boiler and melt. Add 16 marshmallows. Stir. Remove from heat and let cool. Whip cream and add 1/2 to above mixture. Pour into baked pie crust. Use remaining whipped cream on top.

Cinnamon Roll Bread Pudding

This recipe was shared by my Bestie Tari Nixon. Her bread pudding is the yummiest.

3 eggs
1 cup milk
1 teaspoon cinnamon
1/4 cup sugar
4 large cinnamon rolls (scrape off any cream cheese frosting)

Preheat oven to 350 degrees F. Grease baking dish.

Mix eggs, milk, cinnamon, and sugar. Break apart cinnamon rolls. Slowly pour liquid mix over cinnamon rolls.

Bake for 45–60 minutes.

Coca-Cola Pie

Coca-Cola was very popular in the 1950s. Being a newlywed, my mama loved it. Later in life, she loved cooking with it and collected a lot of Coca-Cola paraphernalia. I featured Coca-Cola Cake in my previous book *Faith, Family, Friends & Fried Chicken 2*. I hope you like this Coca-Cola Pie as well. Enjoy.

1 (12-ounce) can Coca-Cola
1/3 cup brown sugar
1/4 cup cocoa powder
1/4 cup cornstarch
4 tablespoons butter
1 teaspoon vanilla
9-inch graham cracker or cookie crust
1 1/2 cups milk chocolate chips
1/2 cup heavy cream

Combine Coca-Cola, brown sugar, cocoa powder, cornstarch, and butter in a saucepan and cook over medium heat. Stir constantly with a whisk for 5-10 minutes or until it gets thick. Remove from heat and stir in vanilla. Pour into pie crust. Cover and place in refrigerator until chilled (about 1 hour).

Melt chocolate chips and cream in microwave in 45-second intervals, stirring after each. Mixture should be creamy and easy to stir. Cool 10 minutes. Spread on top of pie and serve with a dollop of whipped cream and a cherry on top.

Dirty Strawberries

Recipe submitted by my Bestie Tari Nixon, who says,

> The trick is getting everything eaten, with no sour cream or brown sugar left over. It's sort of like trying to even out spaghetti, sauce, and garlic bread. You just keep adding bits until you are about to explode.

My note: *I thoroughly enjoy this recipe, and I have served it at several dinner parties. It would also be a huge hit for your next afternoon tea.*

1 small container sour cream
1 cup brown sugar, not packed
12–15 fresh strawberries

Place a dollop of sour cream in individual saucers. Place spoonful of brown sugar on those same saucers. Place 2–3 strawberries on these saucers.

Have guests dip strawberries into the sour cream, immediately dip them into the brown sugar, and then take a bite. Enjoy the amazing explosion of flavor.

Easy-Peasy Frosting for Cakes

This is so easy, and it makes a very light icing.

1 cup milk
1 small box instant vanilla pudding
1 (8-ounce) package cream cheese at room temperature
1 (12-ounce) carton whipped topping

In a small bowl, whisk together the milk and vanilla pudding, according to directions on pudding box.

In another bowl, whip together cream cheese and whipped topping. Add pudding mixture and mix together.

Refrigerate until chilled, and it's ready to use.

Elvis Presley Cake
(also called Jailhouse Rock Cake)

My Daddy loved Elvis. When he was a young man, he wore white buck shoes and sang Elvis's songs. He had a wavy Elvis thing going on with his hair too. He heard that Elvis ate scoops of vanilla ice cream in halves of cantaloupe, so he tried it. He told me that he became sicker than a dog. Researching the name of this recipe brought back this memory. Hope it brings you a chuckle. I heard the reason that this cake was called Elvis Presley Cake is because he would always ask his grandma to make it for him.

1 box white cake mix
1 (8-ounce) can crushed pineapple
1 cup white sugar
1 (8-ounce) package cream cheese
1/2 cup softened butter
3 cups powdered sugar
1 teaspoon vanilla
2–3 cups crushed pecans

Bake white cake mix according to directions on box, using a 9x13-inch greased pan. Cool and poke holes in it.

Cook crushed pineapple with juice and 1 cup white sugar in saucepan until it boils. Pour over cooled cake.

In a large mixing bowl, combine cream cheese, butter, and powdered sugar. Beat until creamy. Stir in vanilla and crushed pecans. Mix well. Put on top of cake.

Heaven on Earth Cake

This is a really easy and cool dessert for the hot summer months. When I make this, I prefer using strawberry pie filling instead of cherry. I have also made it with blueberry pie filling. They are all great.

1–2 premade angel food cakes
1 (3.4-ounce) package instant vanilla pudding mix
1 1/2 cups 2% milk
1 cup plain Greek yogurt
1 (21-ounce) can cherry pie filling, divided
1 (8-ounce) container Cool Whip, thawed
Crushed pecans (as much as you prefer for garnish)

Cut angel food cake into bite-size cubes.

In a large bowl, whisk together pudding mix and cold milk until thick and well blended. Stir in Greek yogurt.

Spread 1/2 of cake cubes in an even layer in a 9x13-inch baking dish. Top with 2/3 of cherry pie filling. Place remaining cake cubes in and pour pudding mix over the cake. Spread gently to cover. Using a rubber spatula, spread the Cool Whip over the pudding and add the remaining cherry pie filling on top. Garnish with crushed pecans.

Place in refrigerator for at least 3 hours or overnight.

Holy Cow Cake

Holy Cow Cake can be stored covered in the refrigerator for up to one week. It doesn't last that long at my home.

1 box devil's food chocolate cake mix
1/2 cup milk chocolate chips
14 ounces Eagle Brand Sweetened Condensed Milk
1 1/2 cups chocolate syrup
1 1/2 cups caramel sauce
8 full-size Butterfinger candy bars, chopped in small pieces, divided
Holy Cow Cake Frosting

Preheat oven to 350 degrees F.

Mix chocolate cake mix according to the package. Stir in the chocolate chips. Place in greased 9x13-inch baking dish or pan. Bake according to package instructions. Remove from oven. While it is hot, poke holes in cake with a plastic straw. Pour Eagle Brand milk over hot cake and allow it to soak in.

Pour chocolate syrup over cake and allow it to soak in. Pour caramel sauce over cake and allow it to soak in. Sprinkle with 5 chopped Butterfinger candy bars. Spread Holy Cow Cake Frosting on top. Sprinkle with remaining Butterfinger candy bars. Place uncovered in refrigerator for minimum of 30 minutes to chill cake. Cut into squares and serve.

Holy Cow Cake Frosting

1 pint heavy cream
1/4 cup sugar
1 tablespoon instant vanilla pudding mix
1 teaspoon vanilla

Whip the cream, sugar, vanilla pudding mix, and vanilla until it is really thick. Spread frosting all over the cake.

Impossible Coconut Pie

4 eggs
2 cups milk
1 cup coconut (flaked or shredded)
3/4 cup sugar
1/2 cup Bisquick mix
1/4 cup butter, softened
1 1/2 teaspoons vanilla extract

Preheat oven to 350 degrees F. Grease 9-inch pie plate with butter or cooking spray.

Add all ingredients to a blender. Cover and blend on low speed for 3 minutes. Pour into pie plate. Bake 40 minutes. Serve warm.

Joyce's Lemon Pie

This recipe was shared by my beautiful Bestie Tari Nixon, who says that her mom always made this pie for her dad, Tony. It was always his favorite.

1 can sweetened condensed milk
5 egg yolks
1/2 cup lemon juice (from real lemons or bottle)
1 premade graham cracker crust
Whipped cream

Mix condensed milk, egg yolks, and lemon juice (If you want a tarter pie, use a little more lemon juice). Pour into pie shell. Refrigerate (The lemon juice "cooks" the eggs). The pie firms up in a few hours. If for some reason the pie doesn't set, you probably got egg white in the mix when the eggs were separated.

Serve with whipped cream (I only use real whipped cream that I make myself, but already-made whipped cream is a good substitute).

Old-Fashioned Southern Bread Pudding

8 cups 1-inch cubes of day-old French bread
1 1/2 cups raisins
2 cups milk
4 eggs
1 cup sugar
1/4 cup butter, melted
1 teaspoon ground cinnamon
1/2 teaspoon vanilla extract
1/4 teaspoon ground nutmeg
1/8 teaspoon salt

Spray bottom of Crock-Pot with cooking spray.

Place bread and raisins in Crock-Pot.

In a large mixing bowl, whisk together all other ingredients. Pour over bread and raisins. Gently stir to evenly coat the bread. Cover and cook on low heat for 2 1/2 to 3 hours.

Serve warm. Add a dollop of whipped cream on individual servings as a sweet topping.

Peanut Butter Fudge

Recipe submitted by my BFF Jennifer Raskovich, who says, "I use smooth peanut butter, but you could use the crunchy if you like."

2 cups white sugar
1/2 cup evaporated milk
1 1/3 cups peanut butter
1 (7-ounce) jar marshmallow crème

Butter the bottom and sides of an 8-inch pan. Set aside

In a medium saucepan, mix sugar and milk over medium heat. Bring to a full boil, stirring constantly so sugar dissolves and mixture doesn't burn on the bottom of the pan. Boil for 3 minutes, stirring constantly. Remove from heat and add peanut butter and marshmallow crème. Mix well until both are completely melted. Quickly pour into the prepared pan. Chill until set. Cut into squares.

Pecan Pie

My beautiful warrior girlfriend Linda Grossman shared this pecan pie recipe that was her mom's. It's really easy to make and so yummy.

1/8 pound butter
1 cup white sugar
1/4 teaspoon salt
2 eggs. well beaten
1 cup white Karo syrup
1 cup chopped pecans
unbaked 8-inch pie shell

Preheat oven to 325 degrees F.

Cream butter and mix in white sugar. Add the salt, eggs, Karo syrup, and pecans. Mix well. Pour into pie shell. Bake 1 hour.

Pecan Pie Bread Pudding

1 (16-ounce) loaf day-old French bread
4 eggs, beaten
2 1/2 cups milk
1 cup half-and-half
1 cup white sugar
1/8 teaspoon salt
1 tablespoon vanilla
1/2 cup butter, softened
1 1/2 cups packed light brown sugar
1 cup chopped pecans

Preheat oven to 350 degrees F.

Cut bread into bite-size cubed pieces. Place in large bowl.

In separate bowl, beat eggs. Add milk, half-and-half, sugar, salt, and vanilla. Whisk. Pour over bread. Let mixture sit for 15 minutes so bread is moistened.

In a third bowl, combine softened butter, brown sugar, and pecans. Stir with fork until mixture almost looks like wet sand.

Pour half of the bread mixture into an 8x8-inch pan. Top with half the pecan mixture. Spoon remaining bread mixture over the pecan mixture. Top with the remaining pecan mixture. Place pan on cookie sheet (in case it bubbles over) and put in oven.

Bake for 45–55 minutes. Cool until center is set.

Pecan Pie Cake

First Batter

1 box yellow cake mix, except for 2/3 cup
1 stick butter at room temperature
1/2 cup packed light brown sugar
2 large eggs
2 tablespoons water
2 cups chopped pecans

Second Batter

2/3 cup of the yellow cake mix
1 stick butter at room temperature
2 large eggs
1/2 cup white sugar
1/2 cup light corn syrup
1 cup milk
20–25 halved pecans

First Batter

Preheat oven to 325 degrees F.

Put all ingredients except the pecans into a medium mixing bowl. Beat mixture with electric mixer until creamy and thick. Stir in the pecans. Spread into a buttered 9x13-inch baking pan. Bake for 25 minutes.

Second Batter

Put all ingredients into mixing bowl and beat with electric mixer. Batter will be lumpy because of butter, but that's okay.

Remove pan from the oven. Pour second batter over it and return to oven. Bake another 35–40 minutes.

When finished, place halved pecans on top. Serve.

Pistachio Cake

Recipe submitted by my beautiful Bestie Susan Horn. Her husband, Mike, loves to bake this cake. Believe me when I say that it is *so* good. He can bake it for me anytime he wants.

2 small boxes pistachio instant pudding and pie filling
4 eggs
1 box yellow cake mix
3/4 cup oil
3/4 cup water

Preheat oven to 350 degrees F.

Mix all ingredients together. Pour into a Bundt pan. Bake for one hour.

Preacher's Cake

Mama called this Preacher Cake and told me that it got its name many years ago. Most people always had the ingredients in their pantries. If you knew the preacher was coming over, you could make one of these cakes in a hurry.

It was originally made with crushed pineapples. But being raised in a preacher's family, one summer, we were given lots and lots of pineapple cakes (The ladies of the church learned that it was my dad's favorite). So now I can barely look at a pineapple cake. I switched it up to include cinnamon applesauce instead of crushed pineapple. If you prefer to make it the original way, use the pineapple. I won't hold it against you.

3 cups all-purpose flour
2 teaspoons baking soda
1 teaspoon salt
1/2 teaspoon cinnamon
2 cups sugar
3 eggs

1 cup vegetable oil

2 teaspoons vanilla extract

1 (20-ounce) can crushed pineapple (keep the juice)

1 cup flaked coconut

1 1/2 cups finely chopped pecans, divided

Preheat oven to 350 degrees F. Grease a 9x13-inch baking pan.

Sift together flour, baking soda, salt, and cinnamon. Set aside.

Combine sugar, eggs, oil, and vanilla. Mix with electric mixer until creamy. Slowly mix in the flour mixture a little at a time, until everything is combined. Add pineapple with their juice. Add coconut and half the pecans. Mix until thoroughly combined. Pour cake batter into pan and bake 45–50 minutes.

Cool completely. Then frost with Preacher's Cake Cream Cheese Frosting (next recipe). Sprinkle remaining pecans on top. Store in refrigerator.

Preacher's Cake Cream Cheese Frosting

1 (8-ounce) package cream cheese at room temperature
1/2 cup (1 stick) butter at room temperature
1 teaspoon vanilla
2 cups powdered sugar

Whip cream cheese, butter, and vanilla for about 2 minutes or until mixture is fluffy, using an electric mixture on high. Beat in powdered sugar. Add more powdered sugar if you desire a stiffer frosting.

Pumpkin Pie

This recipe was shared by my beautiful warrior girlfriend Linda Grossman. It was her mom's recipe. Linda told me that this recipe makes two pies. She also says her mom never put in the ginger, and everyone always thought her pumpkin pie was the best.

1 teaspoon ginger
2 teaspoons cinnamon
2 cups sugar
3/4 teaspoon salt
1 large can pumpkin
3 eggs
1 can evaporated milk
1 cup whole milk
2 unbaked pie shells

Preheat oven to 450 degrees F.

Mix ginger, cinnamon, sugar, and salt. Add pumpkin and eggs. Blend well. Add evaporated milk and whole milk. Stir until mixed well. Pour into unbaked pie shells.

Bake 15 minutes and then reduce heat to 350 degrees F. for 40 minutes.

Pumpkin Ice-Cream Pie

1 can pumpkin
1/2 cup sugar
1/2 teaspoon salt
1 teaspoon cinnamon
1/2 teaspoon ginger
1/2 teaspoon ground cloves
1 quart vanilla ice cream, slightly softened
1 (9-inch) baked graham cracker pie crust

Combine pumpkin, sugar, salt, cinnamon, ginger, and cloves and mix well. Stir in ice cream and mix with wooden spoon until smooth and blended. Pour into pie shell. Freeze until firm.

Allow to stand at room temperature 10 to 15 minutes before serving.

Recipe submitted by my beautiful warrior girlfriend Carolyn Thompson.

Pumpkin Spice Dump Cake

1 box yellow cake mix
1 teaspoon cinnamon
1/2 teaspoon nutmeg
1/2 teaspoon ginger
1 cup chopped walnuts
1 (15-ounce) can plain pumpkin
1 (14-ounce) can sweetened condensed milk
1 quart vanilla ice cream
1 jar salted caramel topping

Dump yellow cake mix, cinnamon, nutmeg, ginger, and walnuts into a Crock-Pot. Whisk together. Next, dump in pumpkin and sweetened condensed milk. Stir but try not to mix it into the cake mix too much.

Cook on high heart for 2 hours. Stir. Continue cooking for another 2 hours.

When finished, spoon onto dessert plates. Top with vanilla ice cream and drizzle caramel topping over top.

Sex in a Pan Cake

This recipe was submitted by my Bestie Deborah Donnelly, who says,

This recipe was given to us many years ago by a friend of my husband who worked at a resort. It was such a hit and loved by many.

Heavenly. Wowsa! Enjoy.

First Layer

1 cup chopped walnuts
1/2 cup powdered sugar
1 cup flour
1 stick butter

Mix all the above ingredients together to make this crust layer.

Grease a 9-x-13 pan. Bake at 350° F. for 20 minutes. Bake only the first layer. This is the crust.

Second Layer

1 (8-ounce) package cream cheese
1 cup powdered sugar
1/3 cup peanut butter
2 cups Cool Whip (1 container)

Mix all the above ingredients together to make the second layer.

Spread over cooled first layer

Third Layer

3 cups cold milk
1 (3-ounce) package instant chocolate pudding
1 (3-ounce) package instant vanilla pudding

Mix all the above ingredients together to make the third layer. Spread over the second layer.

Top with Cool Whip.

Using a very large chocolate bar, shave chocolate on top of cool whip. Use one medium package of chopped walnuts and add on top too.

S'mores in the Oven

Who says you can't have s'mores on a rainy night while watching your favorite movie?

36 regular-size marshmallows, divided
4 Hershey's milk chocolate candy bars
18 squares honey graham crackers, divided

Preheat oven to 350 degrees F.

Cut marshmallows in half with kitchen scissors. Chop up the candy bars. Place 9 graham cracker squares (single layer) in an 8-inch-square pan. Top with the half of the marshmallows. Add chocolate bars. Cover with remaining graham cracker squares. Top with the second half of the marshmallows (Make sure the cut side is down).

Bake 9–10 minutes or until the marshmallows are puffed and golden brown.

Let stand a few minutes before serving.

Sock It to Me Cake

Cake

1 box of yellow Butter Recipe Cake Mix
3/4 cup vegetable oil
1/2 cup sugar
1 (8-ounce) carton sour cream
4 eggs

Filling

6 tablespoons light brown sugar
1/2 cup chopped pecans
4 teaspoons ground cinnamon

Glaze Icing

1 cup powdered sugar
2 tablespoons butter, melted
2 tablespoons milk
1 teaspoon vanilla

Cake

Preheat oven to 375 degrees.

Mix cake mix, oil, sugar, sour cream, and eggs together. Place about 3/4 of mixture into a greased Bundt pan.

Filling

Mix brown sugar, pecans, and cinnamon together and spread on top of cake mix mixture. Add the remaining cake mix mixture.

Bake 45–55 minutes. Cool about 20 minutes. Remove from pan. Cool completely.

Glaze Icing

1 cup confectioners sugar
1 ½ tablespoon milk

Whisk together the confectioners sugar and milk until creamy.

Then drizzle the Glaze Icing over the cake.

Southern Chess Squares

1 box yellow cake mix
3 eggs, divided
1 stick butter, melted
1 (8-ounce) package cream cheese, softened and
at room temperature
4 cups or 1 (1-pound) box powdered sugar, divided

Preheat oven to 300 degrees F. Grease 9x13-inch
cake pan with butter.

In a medium bowl, mix together cake mix, 1 egg,
and melted butter until it becomes a soft dough.
Spread or press into the bottom of the pan, using
a wooden spoon or spatula.

Using an electric mixer, mix remaining two eggs,
cream cheese, and powdered sugar (Save just
enough to sprinkle on top when done) together
about 2 minutes or until smooth. Pour on top of
the dough in baking pan.

Bake 45–50 minutes and until top is a golden brown. Remove from oven.

Very lightly sprinkle leftover powdered sugar on top before serving. Cut into squares.

Triple Berry Cream Cheese Dump Cobbler

2 cups frozen blackberries
2 cups frozen blueberries
2 cups frozen raspberries
1/4 cup granulated sugar
1 (8-ounce) package cream cheese, cold
1 box yellow cake mix
3/4 cup butter, melted
2 tablespoons powdered sugar
Heat oven to 350 degrees F.

Stir together all three types of berries and cup sugar. Spread evenly on bottom of a 9x13-inch pan. Cut cold cream cheese into cubes. Place cream cheese cubes on top of the berries. Sprinkle dry yellow cake mix over the top of cream cheese. Pour melted butter evenly over top of cake mix.

Bake 50–60 minutes or until the cake is golden brown on top and the edges are bubbling. Cool 10–15 minutes.

Sprinkle with powdered sugar. Serve warm.

Beverages

A lot of the time, drinks are left out and
become afterthoughts to a great meal.

In this chapter, we will not let that happen.
Cheers to my fellow warriors.

Blackberry Iced Tea

5 tea bags (black tea)
4 cups water
1/4 cup crushed mint leaves
1/2 cup sugar (or your favorite sweetener)
2 pounds blackberries

Place tea bags, water, and crushed mint leaves in saucepan and bring to boil. Let steep for 5 minutes on low heat. Pour over a strainer and into a large pitcher. Stir in the sugar. Set aside.

Place blackberries in a blender and puree. Pour over a strainer and into the pitcher of tea. Stir until well blended. Add more sugar to taste. Cover with aluminum foil and place in refrigerator until chilled.

Serve over ice. Place 2–3 blackberries and a mint leaf in each glass to make it pretty.

Brazilian Lemonade

This is my favorite cold summer drink. It's so creamy and yummy. If you want a less bitter and juicier lime, pick the ones with the thinnest, smoothest skins.

6 cups cold water
7–8 tablespoons sweetened condensed milk
4 limes, divided
1 cup sugar (or your favorite sweetener)

Mix water and sugar together until sugar is dissolved. Place in refrigerator.

Wash limes thoroughly. Cut the ends off. Then cut into 8 wedges. Place half the limes and half the sugar water in blender and pulse 4 times. Pour through strainer and into pitcher. Repeat process with the remaining limes and sugar water. Stir in the sweetened condensed milk. Serve over ice.

Easy Hot Chocolate Your Way

Remember, its hot chocolate *your* way.

2 cups milk (use whichever kind you prefer)
1 bag chocolate chips (bittersweet, dark, milk or a combo of all 3)

Place the milk in a medium-size saucepan. Heat on medium heat. Do not boil. Add chocolate chips (however many you want for the flavor you desire). Heat on low heat until thickened and hot, stirring constantly so nothing sticks to bottom of pan. Be careful not to scorch.

Here are some fun things to add for a different taste.

- ✧ Cinnamon and cayenne pepper: These two together make a nice spicy hot chocolate.
- ✧ Espresso powder: The coffee brings out the flavor of the chocolate.
- ✧ Kosher or sea salt: It balances the flavor of the chocolate.

- ✧ Peanut butter: Oh my, a Reese's cup in your cup.
- ✧ Peppermint extract: for that holiday flavor
- ✧ Vanilla extract: brings a vanilla taste to your cup of hot chocolate

Fruit Tea Punch

2 cups granulated white sugar
1 cup water
2 cups tea, brewed strong and cooled
1 cup lemonade
1 cup pineapple juice
2 cups orange juice
1 quart ginger ale
2 cups sliced fresh strawberries

In a saucepan and over medium heat, bring sugar and water to a boil. Continue to simmer until mixture thickens to a thin syrup.

In a large container (punch bowl or gallon jug), combine syrup, tea, lemonade, and juices. Stir well.

Right before serving, add ginger ale. Stir again. Then add the strawberries. Serve chilled or over ice.

Hot Dr. Pepper and Lemon

I have used this easy-peasy recipe for a winter and holiday drink for over forty-give years. It is my all-time favorite winter drink.

1 (16-ounce) bottle Dr. Pepper
1 lemon

Heat Dr. Pepper in a saucepan until bubbly. Wash and slice lemon. Place lemon slice in bottom of a mug. Pour steaming Dr. Pepper over lemon slice.

London Fog

I just love the name of this tea. I mean, you can't get more British than combining tea, fog, and London, right? I researched the name and came to the conclusion that it may have originated with a pregnant woman in Canada, but the creator remains unknown for sure.

1 Earl Grey tea bag
1 cup hot water
1–2 teaspoons raw honey or maple syrup
1/2 cup unsweetened vanilla almond milk
1/4 teaspoon vanilla extract
dash of cinnamon

Place tea bag in mug or pretty teacup. Pour hot water into the cup. Steep for 5 minutes. Add honey or syrup to hot tea.

Use a milk frother to mix together almond milk and vanilla extract. Top tea with frothed milk. Sprinkle dash of cinnamon over top.

Mexican Hot Chocolate

This recipe serves approximately 4–6 people.

Mexican hot chocolate is a little thicker than the usual hot chocolate.

1/3 cup hot water
1 tablespoon powdered cocoa
1/2 (7-ounce) can sweetened condensed milk
4 cups (1 quart) whole milk
4 ounces chopped bittersweet chocolate
1 stick cinnamon
1/2 teaspoon ground cinnamon
1/8 teaspoon nutmeg
1/2 teaspoon chili powder (this is optional)

In a bowl combine hot water and powdered cocoa. Stir until smooth. Place the cocoa mixture into a Crock-Pot. Add the condensed milk, whole milk, bittersweet chocolate, cinnamon stick, ground cinnamon, nutmeg, and chili powder. Heat on low for 2 hours, stirring every half an hour or so.

When finished, serve warm with marshmallows or whipped cream. Sprinkle chocolate shavings on top if desired.

Milk Tea

The half-and-half will swirl around, making your milk tea really pretty before you stir. This is a basic form of tea and the way that I have made my cuppa tea for most of my life.

1 Earl Grey or English Breakfast tea bag
1 cup hot water
1 teaspoon brown sugar to taste
half-and-half to taste

Heat water. Place tea bags in mug or pretty teacup. Pour hot water into cup. Let it steep for 6–8 minutes. Remove tea bag. Add brown sugar and stir to dissolve quickly. Pour in half-and-half. (You can heat half-and-half before you add to hot tea. This helps keep tea hotter longer).

Ocean Water

3 tablespoons granulated sugar
3 tablespoons water
1 teaspoon coconut extract
2 (12-ounce) cans of Sprite
blue food coloring

Heat sugar and water in a small saucepan, stirring until sugar is dissolved and a syrup is made. Pour into pitcher. Stir in coconut extract, Sprite, and food coloring. Serve over lots of ice.

Orange Iced Tea

4 cups brewed tea
1 cup sugar
1 teaspoon vanilla
dash of cinnamon
2 oranges, sliced

Brew tea in saucepan. While still hot, add sugar and stir until dissolved. Add vanilla and cinnamon. Stir. Place half the orange slices in the bottom of a large pitcher. Pour the tea over the orange slices. Stir.

Serve over ice. Cut remaining slices of orange in half. Place one-half orange slice on rim of each glass for garnish.

Parisian Hot Chocolate

(or as the French say, *"Le chocolat chaud"*)

5 ounces bittersweet chocolate bars (best quality
chocolate is a must for this recipe)
2 cups whole milk
couple light shakes of sea salt
2 tablespoons light brown sugar (optional)

Finely chop chocolate.

Using a medium-size saucepan, heat the milk,
stirring to keep milk from sticking to bottom
of pan. Be careful not to scorch. When milk is
warm, remove from heat. Whisk in chocolate.
Whisk until chocolate is melted. Add light
shake or two of sea salt. Return to heat and
bring to a light boil for 2–3 minutes, whisking
constantly (This makes a thicker hot chocolate.
If you desire an even thicker hot chocolate, just

add more chocolate). Add a little brown sugar at a time until it suits your taste (or don't add it at all).

Serve in pretty teacups for a special flair.

Refrigerator Tea

This recipe can also be used for sun tea. Instead of placing in refrigerator, set container outside in the sun all day. I use a large, old glass mason jar that I bought sauerkraut in years ago. It's the perfect size.

4 cups water
3-4 tea bags (black or green tea)

Pour water into a large mason jar or pitcher. Place tea bags in water with strings and labels hanging on outside of jar or pitcher. Cover with lid or aluminum foil. Place in the refrigerator. Steep 6–8 hours or overnight.

Serve over ice. Sweeten to taste.

Southern Summer Peach Tea

(Sherry-Marie's Way)

I love using Sonic ice. You can buy a ten-pound bag of Sonic ice for just two dollars.

Peach Syrup

1 cup sugar
1 cup water
3–4 fresh peaches, sliced

Tea

4 Lipton tea bags
8 cups water

Peach Syrup

Place all syrup ingredients in a saucepan and bring to a boil. Reduce heat to medium and let simmer, stirring until sugar is dissolved and peaches are crushed. Turn off heat and set aside for 30 minutes.

Tea

Place tea bags and water in a saucepan and bring to a boil. Reduce heat to low and let steep for 10 minutes.

Remove tea bags. Drain peaches from the syrup. Add syrup to tea. Stir until well blended. Place in refrigerator to chill.

Serve over ice.

Sparkling Christmas Punch

1 bottle sparkling apple cider
equal parts lemonade and cranberry juice
2 cups frozen raspberries

Stir all ingredients together. Place in pretty punch
bowl or gallon mason jar.

Strawberry Iced Tea

4 cups strawberries (fresh or frozen)
2 cups sugar (or favorite sweetener)
2 cups water
4 cups brewed tea

If using fresh strawberries, wash, cut off tops, and slice. Place strawberries, sugar, and water in a large saucepan. Bring to boil. Reduce heat to low and simmer for 15 minutes. Pour through strainer and into gallon mason jar or pitcher. Pour tea into the pitcher and stir until well blended. Place in refrigerator and chill.

Serve over ice and garnish with half of a strawberry in each glass.

White Hot Chocolate

3 cups milk (whole or 2%)
1 cup half-and-half (or heavy cream)
1 (8-ounce) white chocolate chips
1 1/2 teaspoons vanilla
pinch of salt
marshmallows or whipped cream

In a medium to large pan, add all ingredients except marshmallows and whipped cream. Cook over medium heat. Stir often and until white chocolate chips have melted and hot chocolate is a smooth consistency. Do not bring to a boil.

Serve while hot with marshmallows or whipped cream.

About the Author

Sherry-Marie Perguson is known for her ability to entertain readers with her life stories, which are told in a sassy, southern, and humorous style. She is the author of seven fun and inspirational books:

The *Faith, Family, Friends and Fried Chicken* trilogy
Southern & Sassy ... with a Side of Faith
And Then God Made Chocolate
God, You, and Red Ruby Shoes
Your Crown Slips, So What, Sparkle On

Sherry-Marie continues to spread joy and encouragement to all her readers everywhere. As a speaker, she has held women's conferences, and she is in demand at all types of ladies' events, such as book clubs, coffee groups, and corporate self-help seminars.

Sherry-Marie resides in the Phoenix, Arizona, area. There she has been showcased on Channel 3 *Arizona's Family Morning Show* and featured in the local magazine *85086*.

She is a songwriter and a musician. She has written over seventy songs. Many of them have been recorded on her personal and family albums.

She is a businesswoman. She has owned and operated a highly successful tearoom and a mini antique mall for several years.

But her passion by far is her desire to be an encourager. This explains her quest to become an author.

When asked why she loves writing and speaking so much, Sherry-Marie responded,

> I have fallen in love with my readers. We know life is short and filled with lots of ups and downs. But if I can bring a smile to your face and chuckle from your belly, make you hungry and you get up to cook one of our recipes, and encourage you to keep your faith and know Jesus a little better, I am the most blessed of all women.

Recipe Index

APPETIZERS

BREAKFAST DELIGHTS

THE SIDES

MAIN DISHES AND CASSEROLES

DECADENT DESSERTS

BEVERAGES